SpringerBriefs in Law

SpringerBriefs present concise summaries of cutting-edge research and practical applications across a wide spectrum of fields. Featuring compact volumes of 50 to 125 pages, the series covers a range of content from professional to academic. Typical topics might include:

- A timely report of state-of-the art analytical techniques
- A bridge between new research results, as published in journal articles, and a contextual literature review
- A snapshot of a hot or emerging topic
- A presentation of core concepts that students must understand in order to make independent contributions

SpringerBriefs in Law showcase emerging theory, empirical research, and practical application in Law from a global author community. SpringerBriefs are characterized by fast, global electronic dissemination, standard publishing contracts, standardized manuscript preparation and formatting guidelines, and expedited production schedules

More information about this series at http://www.springer.com/series/10164

Csongor István Nagy

Collective Actions in Europe

A Comparative, Economic and Transsystemic
Analysis

Csongor István Nagy
University of Szeged, Department of Private
International Law
Hungarian Academy of Sciences
Federal Markets "Momentum" Research
Group
Szeged, Hungary

ISSN 2192-855X   ISSN 2192-8568   (electronic)
SpringerBriefs in Law
ISBN 978-3-030-24221-3   ISBN 978-3-030-24222-0   (eBook)
https://doi.org/10.1007/978-3-030-24222-0

This Springer imprint is published by the registered company Springer Nature Switzerland AG
The registered company address is: Gewerbestrasse 11, 6330 Cham, Switzerland

Preface

In the last three decades, Europe has seen a remarkable proliferation of collective action legislation, making class actions one of the most successful export product of the American legal scholarship. While its spread has been surrounded by distrust and suspiciousness, today more than half of the EU Member States have introduced collective actions for damages and, from those who did, more than half chose, to some extent, the opt-out system. This book gives an analytical presentation of how Europe made class actions in its own image. It demonstrates why collective actions have been felt needed from the perspective of access to justice and effectiveness of law and presents the European debate and the deep layers of the European reaction and resistance. It unfolds how the Copernican turn of class actions questions the fundamentals of the European thinking about market and public interest. It analyzes, through a transsystemic presentation of the European national models, the way collective actions were accommodated with the European regulatory environment, the novel and peculiar regulatory questions they had to address and how and why they work differently on this side of the Atlantic.

The author is indebted to Prof. Laura Carballo, Prof. Caroline Cauffman, Prof. Laura Ervo, Dr. Andre Fiebig, Dr. Pavle Flere, Dr. Maciej Gac, Prof. Clifford A. Jones, Prof. Christian Kersting, Prof. Jurgita Malinauskaite, Prof. Francisco Marcos, Prof. Manos Mastromanolis, Prof. Alexandra Mikroulea, Dr. Anton Petrov, Prof. Barry J. Rodger, Dr. Thibault Schrepel, Prof. Caterina Sganga, Prof. Miguel Sousa Ferro, Prof. Astrid Stadler and Dr. Magdalena Tulibacka for their comments. Of course, all views and any errors remain the author's own.

This volume was published as part of the research project of the HAS-Szeged Federal Markets 'Momentum' Research Group. It draws on the author's following publications: Nagy CI (2013) Comparative collective redress from a law and economics perspective: without risk there is no reward! Columbia J Eur Law 19(3): 469–498; Nagy CI (2015) The European collective redress debate after the European Commission's Recommendation: one step forward, two steps back? Maastricht J Eur Compar Law 22(4):530–552. The manuscript was closed on

1 April 2019. Hence, it does not incorporate the Italian legislation adopted on 12 April 2019 (Legge, 12/04/2019 n° 31. Disposizioni in materia di azione di classe (19G00038), GU Serie Generale n. 92 del 18-04-2019).

Szeged, Hungary   Csongor István Nagy

Contents

1 Introduction 1
   References 7

2 Why Are Collective Actions Needed in Europe: Small Claims
   Are Not Reasonably Enforced in Practice and Collective Actions
   Ensure Effective Access to Justice 9
   2.1 What Are the Hurdles Faced by Small Claims in Europe 11
   2.2 How Do Collective Actions Overcome the Above Hurdles
         and Why Are They Efficient? 14
   2.3 Why Are Collective Actions Not Working Spontaneously
         if They Are Efficient? 16
   2.4 How Could Collective Actions Be Made Work?. 17
   2.5 Summary 20
   References 20

3 Major European Objections and Fears Against the Opt-Out
   System: Superego, Ego and Id 23
   3.1 European Objections Against Class Actions: Scruples
         or Pretexts? 23
         3.1.1 Constitutional Concerns: Private Autonomy
                 and Tacit Adherence 24
         3.1.2 Opt-Out Collective Actions Are Alien to Continental
                 Legal Traditions 30
         3.1.3 It Is Very Difficult to Identify the Members of the Group
                 and to Prove Group Membership 33
         3.1.4 Opt-Out Collective Actions Would Lead to a Litigation
                 Boom and Would Create a Black-Mailing Potential for
                 Group Representatives 35

3.2   The Headspring of European Taboos and Traditionalism:
Party Autonomy and the State's Prerogative to Enforce
the Public Interest... 38
3.3   Summary 40
References 42

4   Transatlantic Perspectives: Comparative Law Framing 45
4.1   Disparate Regulatory Environments 45
4.2   Why Should Europeans Not Fear the American Cowboy?
Diverging Effects of Disparate Regulatory Environments 52
4.3   The Novel Questions of Collective Actions in Europe 59
     4.3.1   Funding in the Absence of One-Way Cost-Shifting,
Contingency Fees and Punitive Damages 59
     4.3.2   Two-Way Cost-Shifting 62
     4.3.3   Distrust of Market-Based Mechanisms
in the Enforcement of Public Policy
(No Private Attorney General) 62
     4.3.4   European Opt-In Collective Actions and Joinders
of Parties.. 63
     4.3.5   Opt-Out Systems and the "Only Benefits" Principle...... 64
4.4   Summary 66
References 67

5   European Models of Collective Actions 71
5.1   The European Landscape: To Opt in or to Opt Out?.......... 73
5.2   Purview: Step-by-Step Evolution of a Precautious Revolution 85
5.3   Pre-requisites of Collective Action and Certification 88
5.4   Standing and Adequate Representation 95
5.5   Status of Group Members in Opt-in Proceedings:
Liability for Legal Costs and Res Judicata Effect 98
5.6   Status of Group Members in Opt-Out Proceedings:
Liability for Legal Costs, Res Judicata Effect
and the "Only Benefits" Principle 101
5.7   Enforcement.. 105
5.8   Summary 106
References 108

6   Conclusions 113
6.1   Collective Actions Are Needed in Europe to Ensure Access
to Justice and Effectiveness of the Law 114
6.2   European Objections and Fears Against the Opt-Out System:
Superego, Ego and Id 116
6.3   Transatlantic Perspectives: Comparative Law Framing 117

6.4   European Models of Collective Actions: A Transsystemic
        Overview   119
6.5   Closing Thoughts: "Small Money, Small Football, Big Money,
        Big Football"   121
References   122

Chapter 1
Introduction

Class actions have probably been the most successful export product of the American legal scholarship.[1] While the US legal system does have quite a few peculiarities (such as deterrent punitive and treble damages, extensive pre-trial discovery, constitutionally entrenched jury trials), class actions stand out from these in terms of both intellectual impact and controversial reception. They fulfilled a determinative role, either as a source of inspiration or as a point of reference, in the appearance and evolution of EU collective actions. While a few decades ago collective actions were very rare outside the US and were considered esoteric, nowadays, they are part of the legal systems of Australia and several countries in the Americas (Canada[2] and Latin America[3]) and in Europe, and, even if they happened to reject them, all these systems considered the US class action[4] as the Caballine Fountain and point of reference.

Interestingly, while the spread of collective actions has been remarkable, it has generated the same amount of criticism and fear in Europe[5]: albeit that the class action is certainly not the only legal transplant whose reception divides a legal community, it

---

[1] See Hensler (2017: 965–966).

[2] Several provinces of Canada introduced collective litigation, such as British Columbia, Class Proceeding Act 1995, S.B.C. ch 21 (1995), Ontario, Class Proceeding Act 1992, S.O. ch 6 (1992), Quebec, Quebec Civil Code, Book IX., Newfoundland & Labrador, Class Actions Act, S.N.L., ch. C-18.1 (2001) (Newfoundland & Labrador), Saskatchewan, The Class Actions Act, S.S., ch. C-12.01 (2001) (Saskatchewan). The class action is also part of the Federal Court Rules, Federal Court Rules, Part 4, 299.1–42.

[3] See Gidi (2003: 311, 2012: 901).

[4] For a comprehensive overview of the US class action, see Anderson and Trask (2010).

[5] Cf. Buxbaum (2014: 585, 586) ("In previous decades, the primary flashpoint for friction in cross-border civil litigation was the discovery process (…). Today, the flashpoint for such debates seems to be the class action.").

© The Author(s) 2019
C. I. Nagy, *Collective Actions in Europe*,
SpringerBriefs in Law, https://doi.org/10.1007/978-3-030-24222-0_1

proved to be one of the most controversial. It is not an exaggeration to say that the US class action (as reshaped in 1966)[6] was a "Copernican turn" in civil procedure: while normally the procedure is organized around the claim, in class actions claims are organized around the procedure. Due to this paradigm-shift, class actions interfere with one of the taboos of civil-law—representation without authorization (opt-out rule)[7]—and one of the central principles of societal organization: public policy should be done exclusively by the state and its enforcement cannot be privatized (no "private attorney general").[8]

Not surprisingly, in Europe, few legal reforms have been subject to so much hesitation, scare-mongering and phobia of novel legal solutions as the introduction of collective actions.[9] The entry into force of the Italian law of 2007 on collective proceedings was, due to professional protest, suspended for two years and, at the end of the day, a new act was adopted in 2009.[10] In Hungary, the President of the Republic vetoed an act on collective actions adopted by the Hungarian parliament in 2010 (the act followed the opt-out principle).[11] In July 2009, the conversion of the opt-in scheme into an opt-out system was refused in England and Wales,[12] while recently the opt-out scheme was made available in competition matters, subject to the Competition Appeal Tribunal's discretion.[13]

---

[6]It was the 1966 amendment that effectively introduced opt-out class actions. See Yeazell (1987: 229–232). Beforehand, although opt-in class actions had been available since 1938, class actions had not been a major force. Only the move to the opt-out scheme enabled class actions to become effective and common. Sherman (2003: 130, 132–133).

[7]In the traditionalist opt-in system only those group members are involved in the collective litigation who expressly assent to it, contrary to the "notice and opt-out" system, where silence implies assent and those group members who do not want to get involved have to opt out.

[8]See Hodges (2011), Blennerhassett (2016: 28).

[9]Taruffo (2001: 414) ("[T]he European rejection of class actions—essentially based upon igno-rance—has usually been justified by the necessity of preventing such a monster from penetrating the quiet European legal gardens."). For an overview of the central issues of collective actions in the EU, see Udvary (2013).

[10]Act 244 of 24 December 2007 (Legge 24 Dicembre 2007, n. 244), Act 99 of 23 July 2009 (Legge 23 Luglio 2009, n. 99). See Siragusa and Guerri (2008: 32), Nashi (2010: 147).

[11]See Proposal No T/11332 on the Amendment of Act III of 1952 on the Civil Procedure ("T/11332. számú törvényjavaslat a polgári perrendtartásról szóló 1952. évi III. törvény módosításáról"). As noted above, the proposal was vetoed by the President of the Republic of Hungary.

[12]The Government's Response to the Civil Justice Council's Report, Improving Access to Justice through Collective Actions (2009). See Hodges (2010: 376–379), Hodges (2009: 50–66).

[13]Sections 47A-49E of Competition Act 1998, inserted by Part 1 of Schedule 8 of the Consumer Rights Act 2015.

The EU "federal" regulation of collective actions has also featured a similar oscillation.[14] In October 2009, the European Commission withdrew its proposal for an opt-out system[15] and, after a public consultation carried out one and a half years later and the European Parliament's rejection of the opt-out principle,[16] it finally adopted a non-binding recommendation in 2013 championing the opt-in system and rejecting the most important elements of the US class action.[17] Nonetheless, recently, a rather promising development appeared on the horizon of EU collective actions. In April 2018, the Commission proposed the adoption of a collective action scheme (termed "representative action") in the field of consumer protection law.[18] Although the proposed directive evades the dilemma of opt-in and opt-out through leaving the choice to Member States,[19] it will have an unquestionable virtue: if enacted, it will make consumer collective actions uniformly available in all the Member States.

Both traditionalist conservatism and furious economic lobbying are claimed to have accounted for the foregoing developments. The coalition of these two elements often proved to be unsurmountable. It has not been exceptional to see progressive proposals elaborated in the scholarly laboratories torpedoed by intensive economic lobbying[20] and fail to get through the political filter. In some cases they were fully rejected (for example, in England and Wales in 2009,[21] though, as noted above, recently the opt-out scheme was made available in competition law, subject to the Competition Appeal Tribunal's discretion).[22] In other cases, the initially progressive and effective proposal was emasculated, and the version that was finally adopted was

---

[14]For an overview of EU law's approach as to enforcement in the various sectors, see Faure and Weber (2017).

[15]The text is available in Lowe and Marquis (2014: 511–536). See Ioannidou (2011: 78–80).

[16]European Parliament resolution of 2 February 2012 on "Towards a Coherent European Approach to Collective Redress", (2011/2089(INI)).

[17]Commission Recommendation of 11 June 2013 on common principles for injunctive and compensatory collective redress mechanisms in the Member States concerning violations of rights granted under Union Law. OJ L 201/60. For a general criticism of the Recommendation, see Rathod and Vaheesan (2016: 346–352).

[18]Proposal for a Directive on representative actions for the protection of the collective interests of consumers, and repealing Directive 2009/22/EC, COM(2018) 184 final. See European Parliament legislative resolution of 26 March 2019 on the proposal for a directive of the European Parliament and of the Council on representative actions for the protection of the collective interests of consumers, and repealing Directive 2009/22/EC (COM(2018)0184—C8-0149/2018—2018/0089(COD)).

[19]Article 6.

[20]"There is a strong, well-organized, well-funded and influential opposition to the proposal on class actions". Lindblom (1996: 85), quoted in Välimäki (2007). See Välimäki (2007), Lindblom (2007: 9, 31), Lindblom (2008: 14).

[21]The Government's Response to the Civil Justice Council's Report, Improving Access to Justice through Collective Actions (2009).

[22]The Competition Appeal Tribunal specifies in the collective proceedings order whether the procedure has to be carried out in the opt-in or the opt-out system. Sections 47A-49E of Competition Act 1998, inserted by Part 1 of Schedule 8 of the Consumer Rights Act 2015.

deprived of all the virtues that could make the system workable and widespread (see Finland[23] and France).[24]

This volume gives a transsystemic analysis of European collective actions and an overview of how Europe made class actions in its own image. It addresses collective actions' reception, development and core features and gives a critical analysis of the European approach. This is done through analysing the pivotal regulatory questions from an economic and comparative perspective. Quantitative economic analysis is used to describe the decision-making process of the private actors of litigation (plaintiffs, group representatives and defendants): the actors are dealing with a production process, whose output is litigation, measured by possibly recovered losses.

The book's structure is based on the following pillars.

First, the book gives a law and economics analysis of small claims, demonstrating the need for the introduction of collective actions to secure access to justice and showcasing the benefits of the opt-out scheme. It demonstrates that the central function of collective actions is to tackle the problem of organizational costs, through mitigating and handling the risks attached to them, thus making litigation a possibility in cases that otherwise would not get to court. It argues that the opt-out system tackles the problem of organizational costs in the most efficient manner. Although the group's organizational costs can be reduced through different techniques (for instance, through easing adhesion) and, hence, an opt-in system may also be capable of reducing organizational costs through simplifying the organization of the group, the most cost-effective method is the opt-out system, which is capable of reducing the costs to the minimum (albeit certainly not to zero).

Second, the book addresses and refutes the major arguments and fears against the opt-out system (constitutional inconformity, European traditionalism, exaggerated practical difficulties and the fear of a litigation boom and legal blackmailing potential), inquiring whether these are genuine scruples or pretexts veiling a deeper aversion against class actions. This chapter examines the problem of "representation without authorization" and demonstrates that this is not incompatible either with national constitutional requirements or with European legal traditions. It shows that a collective action system based on the opt-out principle is feasible and would cause no litigation boom and would create no blackmailing potential. It argues that the headspring of Europe's instinctive resistance against American class actions and the subconscious reason why it is so difficult to reconcile the "Copernican turn" of class actions with European traditionalism are the taboo of party autonomy and the state's entrenched prerogative to enforce the public interest.

Third, the book gives an account of the differences between the US and European framework and demonstrates how the disparate regulatory environments entail diverging effects and why and how the European legal and social environment raises

---

[23] Välimäki (2007: 3).

[24] The introduction of collective actions into French law had been examined by two professional committees in the era long before the adoption of the new provisions of the French Consumer Code (Code de la consummation) in 2014. Both committees proposed the introduction of a quasi-opt-out scheme. However, the legislator did not follow any of them. Magnier (2007: 4).

regulatory issues that do not emerge on the other side of the Atlantic. The collective action is a genuine legal transplant in Europe whose comparative analysis has to extend to a large array of framing legal institutions (e.g. contingency fees, American rule of attorney's fees, punitive and treble damages), which need to be addressed to delimit class actions from the operation of unrelated legal doctrines. Furthermore, as a conception fully alien to traditional civil-law thinking, in Europe collective actions raise various questions that do not emerge on the other side of the Atlantic.

This chapter gives an outline of the legal and cultural context of European collective action mechanisms and explains in what this context differs from the environment of US class actions. It demonstrates, through a law and economics comparison between US and European collective actions, that the criticism against the US opt-out class action is not valid if it is applied in Europe. The volume demonstrates that the overgrowths of the US class action are not entailed by the class action itself but rather by the cultural and regulatory environment it operates in; it is the contextual concepts and rules of US law that catalyse the operation of class actions ("American rule" of attorney's fees, punitive damages etc.). It is argued, on the basis of theoretical and empirical considerations, that the overgrowths of the US class action do not come up if this regulatory pattern is applied in Europe.

It is also argued that the effectiveness and widespread use of collective litigation and the potential for abuse and adverse effects are inversely proportional to each other. On the one hand, economically speaking, the group representative's expected income and expected costs cannot be equilibrated in the absence of an appropriate risk premium. On the other hand, such a risk premium would move the European regulatory environment from its current position towards US law. The European legislator or legislators need to find the point of equilibrium where the marginal benefit of effective litigation equals the marginal cost of abuse and adverse effects. Alternatively, they may refuse to provide a risk premium to the group representative; empirical evidence shows that, mainly due to non-economic considerations, collective litigation may also be workable in the absence of a risk-premium, albeit on a low-key level.

Fourth, the volume gives a transsystemic presentation of the European national schemes along the key issues of collective actions: purview (sectoral or general), standing, opt-in and opt-out principle, pre-requisites of collective action, status of group members (whether they are considered parties or non-parties affected by the litigation), legal costs (cost shifting and members' liability) and funding, res judicata effects and enforcement. Collective action legislation is relatively widespread in Europe and plentiful Member States, as well as the European Commission have introduced group proceedings. This chapter demonstrates how Europe's legal tradition shaped the reception of collective actions, showing how European legal systems struggled with accommodating the idea of class action with European legal thinking. It also demonstrates the creative efforts certain European countries made to reconcile representation without authorization (the opt-out rule) with the taboo of party autonomy and the notion that the enforcement of public policy cannot be privatized.

Fifth, in the conclusions, the volume gives an analytical summary and critical evaluation of the emerging European collective action model and submits proposals for the advancement of access to justice and effectiveness of law through collective redress.

This volume examines the collective enforcement of claims for monetary recovery; European mechanisms for non-monetary remedies (such as declaratory judgments, injunctions) fall out of this volume's focus. Accordingly, it deals only with procedures where plaintiffs enforce pecuniary claims. Procedures where a representative plaintiff may seek merely a declaratory judgment or an injunction without having the possibility to claim monetary redress—a pattern that has been available in Europe long since—are not covered.[25] In the same vein, procedural mechanisms where individual actions are coordinated after they have been launched, as well as collective settlement mechanisms, do not come under the focus of the analysis, because, as explained below, they do not advance the collective enforcement of claims. Notably, in the first case (see, for instance, the German Capital Markets Model Case Act) claims are brought individually and then coordinated, implying that the mechanism does not facilitate access to justice through a collective vehicle but coordinates claims that were susceptible of being brought on an individual basis; in the second case, the mechanism cannot be used to enforce the claim but to handle mass cases where the defendant is willing to concede liability. Similarly, for reasons explained below, the use of traditional joinder of parties for handling collective matters, though addressed, does not come under the focus of this book.

In this volume, the term "opt-out system" means that group representatives may institute a collective action without any explicit authorization from the members of the group, who, in turn, may (or may not) leave the group through an express declaration (opt-out). Those who are given notice but do not opt out expressly are considered to be assenting to the procedure. The term "US class action" will be used as the rough equivalent of the opt-out system. The term "opt-in system" means that group representatives may act only on behalf of those group members who explicitly authorized them to do so, i.e. who opted in.

In this volume, "collective action" will be used as a general term referring to group litigation mechanisms at large, while the term class action will refer to the US system. For the sake of simplicity, the economic calculations are based on the assumption that the decision-maker is risk-neutral and use the concept of expected value instead of expected utility. Furthermore, for the sake of simplicity, calculations occasionally assume that in Europe legal costs can be shifted in full to the losing party, disregarding legal and practical hurdles; likewise, they will proceed from the proposition that the plaintiff almost never has a 100% chance to win a case.

---

[25] See e.g. Directive 2009/22/EC on injunctions for the protection of consumers' interests, [2009] OJ L 110/30.

References

Anderson B, Trask A (2010) The class action playbook. Oxford University Press, Oxford

Blennerhassett J (2016) A comparative examination of multi-party actions: the case of environmental mass harm. Hart Publishing, Oxford

Buxbaum HL (2014) Class actions, conflict and the global economy. Indiana J Global Legal Stud 21(2):585–597

Faure M, Weber F (2017) The diversity of the EU approach to law enforcement—towards a coherent model inspired by a law and economics approach. German Law J 18:823–879

Gidi A (2003) Class actions in Brazil—a model for civil law countries. Am J Compar Law 51(2):311–408

Gidi A (2012) The recognition of US class action judgments abroad: the case of Latin America. Brooklyn J Int Law 37(3):893–965

Hensler DR (2017) From sea to shining sea: how and why class actions are spreading globally. Univ Kansas Law Rev 65:965–988

Hodges C (2009) From class actions to collective redress: a revolution in approach to compensation. Civil Justice Quart 28:41–66

Hodges C (2010) Collective redress in Europe: the new model. Civil Justice Quart 29(3):370–395

Hodges C (2011) Objectives, mechanisms and policy choices in collective enforcement and redress. In: Steele J, van Boom WH (eds) Mass justice. Edward Elgar, Cheltenham, pp 101–117

Ioannidou M (2011) Enhancing the consumers' role in EU private competition law enforcement: a normative and practical approach. Competition Law Rev 8(1):59–85

Lindblom PH (1996) Grupptryck mot grupptalan (Group pressure against group action). Svensk Juristtidning 81:85–107

Lindblom PH (2007) National report: group litigation in Sweden, The globalization of class actions. http://globalclassactions.stanford.edu/sites/default/files/documents/Sweden_National_Report.pdf. Accessed 20 April 2019

Lindblom PH (2008) Globalization of class action. National report: group litigation in Sweden. Update paper sections 2.5. and 3. http://globalclassactions.stanford.edu/sites/default/files/documents/Sweden_Update_paper_Nov%20-08.pdf. Accessed 20 April 2019

Lowe P, Marquis M (eds) (2014) European competition law annual 2011: integrating public and private enforcement of competition law—implications for courts and agencies. Hart Publishing

Magnier V (2007) Class actions, group litigation & other forms of collective litigation—France. Global class actions. http://globalclassactions.stanford.edu/sites/default/files/documents/France_National_Report.pdf. Accessed 20 April 2019

Nashi R (2010) Italy's class action experiment. Cornell Int Law J 43:147–173

Rathod J, Vaheesan S (2016) The arc and architecture of private enforcement regimes in the United States and Europe: a view across the atlantic. University of New Hampshire Law Review 14:303–375

Sherman EF (2003) American class actions: significant features and developing alternatives in foreign legal systems. Federal Rules Decisions 215:130–157

Siragusa M, Guerri E (2008) Collective actions in Italy: too much noise for nothing? Global Competition Litigation Rev 1(1):32

Taruffo M (2001) Some remarks on group litigation in comparative perspective. Duke J Constitut Law Public Policy 11:405–421

Udvary S (2013) A kollektív jogorvoslat európai szabályozásának főbb csomópontjai és folyamata. Európai Jog 13(6):1–11

Välimäki M. (2007) Introducing class actions in Finland—lawmaking without economic analysis. http://ssrn.com/abstract=1261623. Accessed 20 April 2019

Yeazell SC (1987) From medieval group litigation to the modern class action. Yale University Press, New Haven

Chapter 2
Why Are Collective Actions Needed in Europe: Small Claims Are Not Reasonably Enforced in Practice and Collective Actions Ensure Effective Access to Justice

It is probably very easy to agree with the tenet that "[r]ights which cannot be enforced in practice are worthless."[1] Small claims face hurdles that may prevent individual enforcement and lead to sub-optimal litigation.[2] While the practical non-enforceabilty of small value claims is often conceived as a question of effectiveness,[3] it also has serious human rights and rule of law implications.[4]

Article 47 of the EU Charter of Fundamental Rights, with reference to legal aid, treats access to justice as part of the right to an effective remedy and to a fair trial.[5] Access to justice is also part of the requirement of rule of law, one of the core values of the EU enshrined in Article 2 TEU.[6]

Furthermore, Member States, due to the principle of loyalty, are obliged to ensure the effective enforcement of EU law. According to Article 4(4) TEU, "Member States shall take any appropriate measure, general or particular, to ensure fulfilment of the obligations arising out of the Treaties or resulting from the acts of the institutions of the Union." According to the CJEU's judicial practice, Member States' enforcement of EU law is subject to two general requirements: the principle of equivalence and the principle of effectiveness. National rules governing the enforcement of EU law may not be less favorable than those governing similar domestic actions

---

[1] European Commission Staff Working Document Public Consultation: Towards a coherent European approach to collective redress, SEC (2011) 173 final, para 1.1.

[2] For a detailed elaboration of the analysis set forth in this section, see Nagy (2013: 469–498).

[3] See Neumann and Magnusson (2011: 154–155), Juska (2014), Bosters (2017: 17).

[4] For an overview of the intersection between collective actions and human rights, in particular access to justice, see Hodges (2008: 187–192), Lange (2011: 95–106), Neumann and Magnusson (2011: 151–152), Wrbka et al. (2012), Azar-Baud (2012: 15, 17–18), Vanikiotisa (2014: 1643–1644), Mulheron (2014: 52–57).

[5] "Legal aid shall be made available to those who lack sufficient resources in so far as such aid is necessary to ensure effective access to justice."

[6] European Union Agency for Fundamental Rights and Council of Europe (2016: 16).

© The Author(s) 2019
C. I. Nagy, *Collective Actions in Europe*,
SpringerBriefs in Law, https://doi.org/10.1007/978-3-030-24222-0_2

(principle of equivalence) and they may not make the enforcement of EU law practically impossible or excessively difficult.[7]

Not surprisingly, the Commission's Recommendation on Collective Redress defines collective actions as a means to "facilitate access to justice in relation to violations of rights under Union law" and to reinforce the effectiveness of EU law.[8]

> The purpose of this Recommendation is to facilitate access to justice, stop illegal practices and enable injured parties to obtain compensation in mass harm situations caused by violations of rights granted under Union law, while ensuring appropriate procedural safeguards to avoid abusive litigation.[9]

The Recommendation is based on the premise that collective actions enhance both the effectiveness of the law (through stopping and deterring unlawful practices) and the chance to obtain a real legal remedy (compensation).

> These measures are intended to prevent and stop unlawful practices as well as to ensure that compensation can be obtained for the detriment caused in mass harm situations. The possibility of joining claims and pursuing them collectively may constitute a better means of access to justice, in particular when the cost of individual actions would deter the harmed individuals from going to court.[10]

This chapter demonstrates how and why collective actions make the enforcement of small value claims a reality, thus ensuring access to justice and effectiveness of the law. It addresses three questions: why is the practical enforcement of small value claims difficult or even unfeasible, how do class actions make it work and why can class actions not become a reality without legislative intervention?

In case of small-value claims it may be economically unreasonable to litigate (the expected costs may be higher than the expected value) even in well-founded cases of merit. First, non-recoverable legal costs may deter litigation. Although in Europe legal costs are, in principle and with some restrictions, borne by the losing party, the winning party cannot shift the legal costs in full. Second, the costs of the preliminary legal assessment may also dissuade the plaintiff. Third, in the context of small claims, the value at stake is small and legal costs are, in comparison to the claim's value, very high—here, a relatively trivial probability of failure may make the balance of litigation negative. The higher the legal costs are in relation to the claim's value, the better this risk crops out.

Collective actions have certain advantages that make the enforcement of small claims possible in cases where numerous persons are damaged by the same illegal act. Although damages are small for each individual (which may make litigation unreasonable), collective damages (the sum of various individuals' damages) are high. The merit of collective actions can be attributed to two virtues: economies of

---

[7] See e.g. Case C-261/95 *Palmisani* [1997] ECR I-4025, para 27; Case C-453/99 *Courage and Crehan* [2001] ECR I-6297, para 29; Joined Cases C-295/04 to C-298/04 *Manfredi* [2006] ECR I-06619, para 62.

[8] Recitals (1) & (10).

[9] Para 1.

[10] Recital (9).

scale[11] and tackling external economic effects (externalities). These are due to the fact that the enforcement of individual small claims may have significant common costs[12] and individual litigation may entail positive external effects (externalities), conferring advantages on other class members they did not pay for.

Although group members could avail themselves of various traditional legal tools (joinder of parties,[13] assignment of claims to an entity founded by group members) to organize the group,[14] these are, at leat in case of small claims, not effective substitutes of collective actions owing to the costs of group organization. These costs may be very high, in some cases even prohibitive,[15] and traditional legal tools are not tailored to the needs of collective litigation, thus increasing the costs of group management.[16]

For the purpose of the present volume, small claims are defined as civil claims where the litigation's expected value is less than its expected costs (out-of-pocket expenses and related inconvenience). At this point, for the sake of simplicity, it is disregarded that the same value (pay-out) may have different utilities for people with different assets and personal preferences (expected utility); likewise, it is assumed that the decision-maker is risk-neutral. When calculating the expected value, it is to be taken into account that litigation is burdened by dubiety and the outcome, in terms of practice, cannot be predicted with full certainty. Hence, a rational decision-maker makes his choice whether to enforce the claim or not on the basis of the balance of litigation's expected value (which stands for the revenue if carrying the day multiplied by the probability that the plaintiff wins the law-suit) and expected costs. If the expected value exceeds the expected costs, it is reasonable to sue.

2.1 What Are the Hurdles Faced by Small Claims in Europe

In Europe, there are essentially three factors that may discourage potential plaintiffs from enforcing their claims: the "loser pays" principle does not work to the full (there are some legally unrecoverable expenses and there are some expenses that cannot be proved), the costs of the preliminary legal assessment and the risk of losing the law-suit (legal and factual uncertainties and dubiety related to the law-suit's outcome; i.e. the risk of bearing the legal costs).

---

[11]See e.g. Ulen (2011: 185, 187).

[12]See Bone (2003: 261–265).

[13]Nagy (2011: 163), Geiger (2015: 32–73).

[14]See Commission Report on the implementation of the Commission Recommendation of 11 June 2013 on common principles for injunctive and compensatory collective redress mechanisms in the Member States concerning violations of rights granted under Union law (2013/396/EU), COM(2018) 40 final, p 2 ("In the Member States where (…) [collective redress mechanisms] do not formally exist there appears to be an increasing tendency of claimants attempting to seek collective redress through the use of different legal vehicles like the joinder of cases or the assignment of claims.").

[15]Ulen (2011: 185, 191).

[16]For a detailed analysis, see Nagy (2013: 469, 478–479).

First, legal costs may deter litigation. As in Europe legal costs are, in principle and with some restrictions, borne by the losing party, the advancing of legal costs should, theoretically, not impede the enforcement of well-founded claims, if assuming that there is 100% probability that the plaintiff wins the law-suit. Nevertheless, in practice, this is seldom the case. The winning party cannot shift the legal costs in full onto the losing party: the proof and documentation of the legal costs may be difficult; furthermore, the law may restrict the amount of the attorney's fees that can be shifted on the losing party; finally, the preliminary legal assessment, examining the probability of plaintiff success, occurs in a stage where the plaintiff has little information about his chances.

Litigation gives rise to some practically unrecoverable expenses; these are to be borne by the plaintiff irrespective of whether he carries the day or not (de facto non-shiftable costs). There are certain costs that may be legally shifted but cannot be proved. Since in this regard the burden of proof rests on the plaintiff, he inevitably faces some risk of proof emerging from factual uncertainties. It is not realistic to assume that the party can prove all his costs before the court, since smaller expenses may not be certifiable. In the context of small claims even relatively negligible expenses may be significant.

Furthermore, there are certain costs that legally cannot be shifted onto the losing party (de jure non-shiftable costs): e.g. inconveniences related to litigation, the time the plaintiff spends on the law-suit. One subset of this category is capped costs. For instance, in certain European countries the law establishes the maximum amount of attorney's fees that can be shifted on the losing party, while the market price of attorney services may be much higher.[17] The usual perception is that the price of attorney services is unregulated and the legally determined schedule of attorney's fees sets out lower fees than the market price. In this case the law, due to the schedule of attorney's fees, enables the plaintiff to shift his attorney's fees only in part. In other civil-law systems, there is no pre-determined schedule of attorney's fees that can be shifted on the losing party but the law authorizes the court to control the fees and it may reduce the amount that can be shifted, if the attorney's fees are not proportionate to the work done or the value of the claim.[18] Accordingly, the plaintiff faces some uncertainty as to whether the attorney's fees will be shifted at the end of the day.

Second, the expenses of the preliminary legal assessment may also discourage the plaintiff. These consist of the information costs of learning whether the plaintiff has a "good case" and how high the risk of losing the law-suit is. Here, the legal counsel assesses the fact pattern and gives advice as to whether to sue and what the potential outcomes of the law-suit are. Although these are costs that emerge in the litigation process broadly speaking and, as such, the winning party may be able to shift them onto the loser, it should not be disregarded that there is a good deal of information shortage in such scenarios. Laymen themselves may not be able to do the preliminary

---

[17] See the case of Germany: Rechtsanwaltsvergütungsgesetz vom 5. Mai 2004 (BGBl. I S. 718, 788), zuletzt geändert durch Artikel 3 des Gesetzes vom 8. Juli 2006 (BGBl. I S. 1426). On the German system, see Wagner (2009: 367).

[18] See the case of Hungary: Regulation 32/2003 (VIII. 22.) of the Minister of Justice.

legal assessment of their chances in a law-suit and, hence, when they are asking for a legal advice they have to take into account that they may have to pay the costs of the preliminary legal assessment even in a case when there is no reason to sue. Thus, in case of small claims, the expenses related to the preliminary legal assessment may have a discouraging effect because the party has to incur costs without knowing the probability of whether they will be recovered or not.

Third, litigation inevitably involves some risk. As a matter of practice, almost all law-suits have immanent risks; a claim may be a good case but seldom a perfect one, let alone the risks emerging from enforcement issues and the defendant's possible insolvency. Accordingly, the party has to take into account that there is a certain risk (even if a negligible one) that he loses the case and, hence, his legal costs would not be recovered and he has to reimburse the opposing party for his expenses.

As in case of small claims the value at stake is small, a relatively trivial probability of failure may make the balance of litigation negative. Assume that the plaintiff suffered € 100 loss due to a bank's overcharge and the legal costs would be € 10,000 altogether; it is also assumed that the claim is fully legitimate but the plaintiff considers that there is a 1% chance that he would lose the case; finally, for the sake of simplicity, it is also assumed that all legal costs are borne by the losing party (no restrictions apply, neither legal, nor factual). In this case, the expected value of the law-suit is € $100 \times 0.99 = $ € 99, while the expected costs are € $10,000 \times 0.01 = $ € 100. As a corollary, the balance of litigation is negative (€ $99 - $ € $100 = $ € $- 1$) and it is not reasonable to sue. Accordingly, a negligible amount of risk may hinder the plaintiff from the law-suit, if legal costs are high in relation to the claim's value. The higher the legal costs are in relation to the claim's value, the better this risk crops out.

It needs to be added that, as a matter of practice, litigation usually involves some risk, even if a negligible one. Furthermore, there is always a risk that even though the court decides for the plaintiff, the enforcement of the judgment fails for some reason (e.g. the judgment debtor becomes bankrupt).

The consequence of the above is that in matters where numerous victims suffer individually small damages they are not seeking recovery on an individual basis and the only legal tool that, in terms of practice, remains at their disposal is public enforcement, e.g. administrative law, criminal law. Nonetheless, public enforcement normally does not imply private recovery[19]: no recovery accrues to the victim from the criminal or administrative sanction imposed on the person committing the mischief.[20]

Accordingly, the conclusion may be drawn that in case of small claims the balance of the expected value and the expected costs may be negative also in cases that should be worth being brought before court, i.e. in cases that have a robust chance of success.

---

[19]For an exception to this general tenet, see Nagy (2012) (Demonstrating how the Hungarian Competition Office uses commitment procedures to further remedies under private law.).

[20]*Contra* Wagner (2011: 79) (Arguing that in case of scattered loss (small claims), the function of collective redress is deterrence.); see also Gilles and Friedman (2006: 105) (Arguing that the purpose of US consumer class actions is not to ensure compensation; instead, its sole purpose is deterrence.).

2.2 How Do Collective Actions Overcome the Above Hurdles and Why Are They Efficient?

In the following, it is demonstrated that collective actions have certain merits that enable the enforcement of small claims in matters where numerous persons suffer loss due to the same mischief (individual loss is small and, hence, as a matter of practice, hardly enforceable, while the sum of the individual losses is high). The two main reasons of this virtue are economies of scale[21] and tackling the problem of external economic effects (externalities).

Collective litigation may lead to economies of scale. There are common costs between the claims and their joint enforcement may give rise to economies of scale and help avoiding externalities that individual litigation may entail[22]; of course these merits may be present not only in respect of small claims.

In related matters sharing common factual and legal issues, litigation costs are usually not directly proportionate to the number of the parties (plaintiffs). If the claims are tried in one action, witnesses have to testify only once and, similarly, liability is to be deliberated only once.[23] Accordingly, if the attorney's workload is 10 h in relation to one client, this may, in case of 100 clients, be 100, 200 or 300 h but not 1000 h. A substantial part of the legal costs, including attorney's fees, may be fixed costs, i.e. they emerge irrespective of the number of the parties, while the rest is made up of variable costs, the volume of which depends on the number of the parties. There are certain issues whose analysis is independent of the number of the parties, while some other (factual and legal) issues are individual and cannot be shared. The ratio between the fixed and variable costs depends on the circumstances; nevertheless, it may be reasonably concluded that if the detriment suffered by the victims is due to the same cause, common (fixed) costs are likely to exist and if the fixed costs are substantial in relation to individual costs, collective litigation may be cost-effective.

Assume that there are 10 victims, each of them suffered damages in value of € 1000 and the costs of individual litigation are € 750 for the plaintiff and the defendant, respectively, € 500 of which is fixed costs (at this point court fees, inflation and interest on overdue payments are disregarded). Furthermore, assume that the plaintiff has 50% chance to win the law-suit because this is a case of first impression raising legal questions that have not been tried before. In case of individual litigation, the balance of the expected value and the expected costs is the following: the expected value is € 500 (€ 1000 × 0.5), while the expected costs are € 750 (since the "loser pays" principle applies, there is 50% chance that the plaintiff has to sustain the legal costs of both parties: [2 × € 750] × 0.5), assuming that legal costs can be perfectly calculated and shifted. Accordingly, the balance is negative (€ 500 − € 750 = € − 250) and it is not reasonable to sue.

---

[21] See e.g. Ulen (2011: 185, 187).
[22] See Bone (2003: 261–265).
[23] Ulen (2011: 187).

Nonetheless, the balance is positive in case of collective litigation, provided certain costs can be shared.[24] If all the 10 victims sue jointly, legal costs do not increase considerably. The costs on the plaintiffs' side are € 500 common fixed costs and € 250 individual variable costs multiplied by the number of group members (€ 250 × 10 = € 2500); altogether, this is € 3000. For the sake of simplicity, assume that the legal costs on the defendant's side do not change: € 750. As a corollary, the total sum of the legal costs is € 3750 and the expected costs are € 3750 × 0.5 = € 1875. On the other hand, the expected value decuples: € 1000 × 0.5 × 10 = € 5000. Under such circumstances, it is reasonable to sue, since the balance of the expected value and the expected costs is positive (€ 5000 − € 1875 = € 3125).

This calculation assumes linear variable costs (no economies of scale due to variable costs); however, part of the variable costs may be degressive, making the total cost of the joint production of collective action on the plaintiffs' side less than € 3000. For example, € 100 may be linear, resulting in costs of € 1000, while € 150 of the variable costs may be degressive and increase not 10 times but only 7 times, so the total costs would amount to € 500 + € 1000 + € 1050 = € 2550. Under such circumstances, it is even more reasonable to sue. The legal costs on the defendant's side do not change: € 750. The total sum of legal costs is € 3300, hence, the expected costs are € 3300 × 0.5 = € 1650. The expected value remains unchanged: € 1000 × 0.5 × 10 = 5000 EUR. Under such circumstances, it is reasonable to sue, since the balance of the expected value and the expected costs is positive (€ 5000 − € 1650 = € 3350).

Another problem of individual enforcement of similar or identical claims emerging from the same cause is that individual litigation may entail significant positive externalities on fellow-sufferers. The litigation's "expected cost – expected value" balance may be negative on individual level but positive on group (or social) level. Since the positive external economic effect conferred on other group members is not internalized by the individual litigator, this may lead to suboptimal enforcement. This happens in test cases, which could be regarded as an alternative to collective actions. Here, one of the group members, as a pioneer, institutes an individual action in a matter that involves a question (or several questions) relevant for all group members. Once the question becomes judicially settled in the test case, this entails a positive externality on all other group members suing afterwards: since the court answers one of the crucial questions in the test case, the litigation risks of other group members decrease. Unfortunately, test cases are not an effective substitute of collective litigation. One of the reasons is that they may lead to free-riding: non-active group members free-ride on the efforts of the member initiating the test case. Collective actions may tackle the positive externality problem through internalizing all or most of the benefits of the law-suit and, thus, leading to socially optimal private enforcement.

At the same moment, not only positive but also negative external effects may be present here; if group members sue on an individual basis and the defendant wins against the first plaintiff, this may have a negative impact on subsequent plaintiffs.

---

[24]Ulen (2011: 266).

Although the judgment given in the case of one of the group members has no res judicata effect in actions brought by other group members, the judgment in the first case may have precedential value or at least persuasive authority. Hence, the defendant may find it rational to invest much more in winning the early cases, because winning in these proceedings may discourage subsequent litigation.[25]

Likewise, collective actions may be cost-effective also for courts. Economies of scale are present here too. Of course, it is to be noted that if individual litigation would not occur due to the above hurdles and inconveniences, collective litigation may actually entail extra-costs for courts, since it may bring matters before the judiciary that would otherwise not be litigated. Nevertheless, this cost-saving is not due to cost-effectiveness but reveals that collective actions may enable the litigation of claims that would otherwise, due to practical hurdles, not come before the judiciary.

2.3 Why Are Collective Actions Not Working Spontaneously if They Are Efficient?

Having demonstrated that collective litigation may be more efficient than individual enforcement, the question emerges: why do group members not organize the group proceedings themselves? European legal systems provide for both substantive and procedural tools that could be used for collective litigation. Group members may establish an entity (a company or association) and assign their claims to this entity.[26] They may also establish a joinder of parties and sue jointly.[27]

The answer lies primarily in the costs of group organization.

First, these costs may be very high, even prohibitive[28], in case of small-claims. Furthermore, the traditional legal tools that could be used to organize the group were essentially not tailored to the needs of collective actions, thus increasing the costs of organization. For instance, in case of a joinder of parties, individual group members may have different legal representatives and may make pleadings that contradict each other. A joinder of parties does not "centralize" the group; it simply enables group members to be part of the same law-suit and to sit on the same side.

Second, the costs related to the organization of the group may not be or may not be easily shifted. The "loser pays" principle relates to legal costs, and the concept of legal costs may not be tailored to organizational expenses; hence, group representatives may not expect reimbursement for these. Most European systems provide that the losing party pays the costs of the proceedings; however, the expenses related to the organization of the group emerge prior to the proceedings and, hence, their status,

---

[25]Ulen (2011: 189).

[26]Nagy (2011: 16).

[27]Nagy(2011: 163).

[28]Ulen (2011: 191, 2012: 79).

in this system, is dubious. The group's organizer (representative) may not expect a reasonable return on his expenses, as within the group he may enforce only his claim.[29]

Third, organizational costs qualify as transaction costs[30]: they emerge also in case the organization of the group fails and, hence, the collective action is not launched at all. Since the stake of individual group members is small, they would not invest in organizing the group due to the same reasons they do not engage in individual litigation.

Fourth, even if group organizers had the right to claim reimbursement for the organizational costs, the same risk would be involved here as in case of legal costs: cost-shifting occurs only if the plaintiff wins, while organizational expenses emerge irrespective of the outcome of the collective action.

2.4 How Could Collective Actions Be Made Work?

There are different methods, which could be used to tackle the problem of high organizational costs. These either reduce organizational expenses or tackle the risks attached to them.

First, opt-out systems are associated with considerably lower organizational costs.[31] Organizational costs may be reduced significantly through providing that group members do not have to join the group explicitly to become part of the collective action; it is sufficient if they do not leave the group (opt-out). In this case, essentially, the group does not need to be organized, since power of attorney is conferred on group representatives by the law, albeit some organizational costs may emerge. Empirical evidence shows that, not surprisingly, the rate of participation is much higher in opt-out collective proceedings than in opt-in actions.[32]

Second, organizational costs may be mitigated even if the opt-in system is adopted. Although traditional joinder of parties and assignment of claims have always been available for group litigation, these entail considerable organization and case-

---

[29] Silver (2000: 206–207).

[30] See Footnote 25.

[31] Cf. Delatre (2011: 38) (Submitting that the opt-out collective action would be sufficient "on its own and without further incentives to lead to a substantial increase in the number of victims compensated."); Szalai (2014: 708–709).

[32] See Mulheron (2008) 147–156 (A study of jurisdictions where modern empirical data existed showed that opt-out rates had been between 0.1 and 13%; in respect of jurisdictions where such data was not available, judicial summations indicated an opt-out rate between 0 and 40%. On the other hand, in Europe, the experience indicated that the rate of participation, that is opt-in, was on average less than 1% in large size collective proceedings, albeit in England and Wales participation rate in group litigation varied considerably, from less than 1% to almost 100%.); Delatre (2011: 38) ("It is (…) submitted that, in a bundle of similar incentives regarding the cost of the action, damages and legal fees, the opt-out arrangement of a class action invariably includes more participants that the alternate opt-in arrangement, as for equal incentives, the rate of rational apathy of victims will always be higher than the rate of victims who opt-in.").

management costs. A traditional joinder of parties is far from equal to an opt-in collective action. In case of the former, individual group members retain their rights over their own cases: they may make submissions independently from the rest of the group, even if this thwarts the legal tactics of the group representative. In case of an opt-in collective action, the group representative, though supervised by the court, becomes the master of the case. Furthermore, in the opt-in system, organizational costs may be further mitigated through the simplification of group organization (e.g. simplifying the administrative burdens and formal requirements related to declarations of adherence).[33]

Third, the problem of organizational costs may be mitigated also through an effective cost-shifting mechanism: if extending the "loser pays" principle to organizational costs, successful group representatives would be entitled to claim remuneration for their reasonable organizational expenses.

Fourth, this extension of the notion of "legal costs" would not be sufficient to make collective actions work, because group representatives would still run the risk of not being reimbursed for their organizational efforts in the event they fail to organize the group properly (group members do not authorize them in a sufficient number in an opt-in system) or the probability of plaintiff success is less than 100% (which is normally the case). Individual litigation involves two parties (i.e. the plaintiff and the defendant), and when the plaintiff considers whether to sue or not to sue (that being the question), he obviously takes into account the income accruing to him if the claim is successfully enforced. Collective litigation involves a third actor as well: the group representative, who has to draw his own individual balance of whether to sue or not to sue; however, the group representative may not expect any income (or only a small income, if he is also a group member) from the claims enforced. The individual plaintiff may regard it reasonable to take the risk of not being reimbursed for his legal costs and of being liable for the legal costs of the defendant, because he knows that if he wins, he will get what he sues for. On the other hand, the group representative has no individual stake in the claim or his claim as a group member is incomparably smaller than the costs and risks he assumes in the interest of the group. The "loser pays" rule and the inclusion of the organizational costs in its scope imply that the group representative *may be* reimbursed for his expenses; however, these do not imply that he *will be* reimbursed.

Therefore, it is not economically rational for the group representative to engage in group organization in the absence of an appropriate risk premium, which—as a general principle—is not afforded to him in Europe.[34] While group representatives

---

[33] For a discussion on how complicated it may be to handle a bulk of complaints, see Patetta (2010).

[34] See Hodges (2010: 373) ("In simple terms, a judicial collective damages procedure will only be effective if there exist both an aggregating procedure and liberal financial rules, such that parties (or more likely their lawyers) will have sufficient economic incentives to find it attractive. Ironically, a collective judicial procedure without attractive financial returns for intermediaries will not deliver the policy objectives, but as the financial returns increase, so does the risk of abuse, and adverse consequences become inevitable."); Cf. Leskinen (2011: 112) ("[T]he possibility of large contingency fees provides incentives to lawyers to bring damages actions and is an essential prerequisite of the functioning of the class action mechanism, in particular, when the individual claims are small").

may have non-economic interests in organizing the group (as civil organizations usually have), economically speaking, the group representative's expected income and expected costs cannot be equilibrated in the absence of an appropriate risk premium.

An alternative solution could be if group members contributed to the organizational costs through paying a fee when joining the group (member contributions). Nonetheless, this solution seems to be both legally unfeasible in opt-out collective proceedings and economically inefficient. First, opt-out collective proceedings may raise constitutional concerns in Europe because they establish power of attorney without authorization.[35] The main argument against these concerns is that the opt-out mechanism is justified, because it confers solely advantages on group members[36]: if the group representative wins, group members receive redress, if he fails, group members do not have to pay anything.[37] This argument would be lost and constitutional concerns would emerge if group members were held liable for the costs of an action they did not expressly consent to. Second, demanding a contribution from members would be inefficient because it would place the litigation risk on the less informed party. Theoretically, the risk of litigation may be placed either on the group representative or on group members. Group representatives are in the best position to assess the probable outcomes and the risks of the proceedings; hence, it is reasonable to place the risk of litigation on them, compensating them for this hazard through an appropriate risk premium.

The above reasoning holds true also for traditional legal costs. Under the general principle, group members should advance their legal costs and should reimburse the defendant for his legal costs if he wins. Alternatively, at least as to opt-out proceedings, the same constitutional and economic arguments may be applied here as in case of organizational costs. Cost-bearing in case of power of attorney without authorization (that is, opt-out collective actions) may raise constitutional concerns; furthermore, the group representative is in the best position to assess the potential risks attached to litigation, thus, it is more efficient to place this risk on the group representative and to provide him with an appropriate risk premium.

In summary, in order to make collective actions workable, measures are to be taken in two directions. Organizational costs should be lessened and the risk of not being reimbursed for the legal costs and of being held liable for the legal costs of the defendant should be tackled through an adequate risk premium.

---

[35] See Leskinen (2011: 87). For France, see e.g. Conseil Constitutionnel Decision No. 89–257DC, 25 July 1989 (Fr.), reproduced in Magnier and Alleweldt (2008) For Hungary, see e.g. Hungarian Constitutional Court's decisions in Alkotmánybíróság (AB) (Constitutional Court) 4 January 1994, 1/1994. (I. 7.); Alkotmánybíróság (AB) (Constitutional Court) 17 April 1990, 8/1990. (IV. 23.).

[36] See Stuyck (2009: 491), Ioannidou (2011: 79–80).

[37] On the argument that collective proceedings improve access to justice, see Ioannidou (2011: 71–73).

2.5 Summary

This chapter described the hurdles that may prevent the individual enforcement of small claims and lead to suboptimal enforcement. It was demonstrated that collective litigation is more efficient in several ways than individual enforcement, and in numerous cases it is the only feasible enforcement mechanism. Given that they generate economies of scale and tackle the problem of positive externalities, collective actions may be a reasonable possibility also in cases where the costs of individual action are prohibitively high.

Having shown that in certain cases collective litigation is more efficient, it was asserted that the absence of the spontaneous emergence of collective actions is chiefly due to the costs of group organization, which qualify as transaction costs and normally cannot be shifted onto the losing defendant. Since organizational costs are crucially important, the regulation should primarily address this issue.

Organizational costs could be considerably lessened with the introduction of the opt-out system. In the opt-in system, the problem of organizational costs could be mitigated through the simplification of group organization (e.g. simplifying the administrative burdens and formal requirements related to declarations of adherence). Irrespective of whether an opt-out or an opt-in system is chosen, organizational costs should be included in the scope of the "loser pays" cost-shifting rule (the losing defendant should be obliged to reimburse the group representative not only for legal costs but also for organizational costs).

For the group representative, it is economically rational to engage in group organization only in exchange for an appropriate risk premium, which is not afforded under the general principles of civil procedure in Europe. Economically speaking, the group representative's expected income and expected costs cannot be equilibrated in the absence of an appropriate risk premium.

References

Azar-Baud MJ (2012) La nature juridique des actions collectives en droit de la consommation. Revue européenne de droit de la consommation 1:3–28

Bone R (2003) Civil procedure: the economics of civil procedure. Foundation Press

Bosters Th (2017) Collective redress and private international law in the EU. TMC Asser Press, The Hague

Delatre JG (2011) Beyond the White Paper: rethinking the Commission's Proposal on Private Antitrust Litigation. Competition Law Review 8(1):29–58

European Union Agency for Fundamental Rights and Council of Europe (2016) Handbook on European law relating to access to justice. http://fra.europa.eu/en/publication/2016/handbook-european-law-relating-access-justice. Accessed on 20 April 2019

Geiger C (2015) Kollektiver Rechtsschutz im Zivilprozess: Die Gruppenklage zur Durchsetzung von Massenschäden und ihre Auswirkungen. Mohr Siebeck, Tübingen

Gilles M, Friedman G (2006) Exploding the class action agency costs myth: the social utility of entrepreneurial lawyers. University of Pennsylvania Law Review 155:103–164

Hodges Ch (2008) The reform of class and representative actions in European Legal Systems. Hart Publishing, Oxford

Hodges C (2010) Collective redress in Europe: the new model. Civil Justice Quart 29(3):370–395

Ioannidou M (2011) Enhancing the consumers' role in EU private competition law enforcement: a normative and practical approach. Competition Law Rev 8(1):59–85

Juska Z (2014) Obstacles in European competition law enforcement: a potential solution from collective redress. Eur J Legal Stud 7(1):114–139

Lange S (2011) Das begrenzte Gruppenverfahren: Konzeption eines Verfahrens zur Bewältigung von Großschäden auf der Basis des Kapitalanleger-Musterverfahrensgesetzes. Mohr Siebeck, Tübingen

Leskinen C (2011) Collective actions: rethinking funding and national cost rules. Competition Law Rev 8(1):87–121

Magnier V, Alleweldt R (2008) Country report: France. In: Evaluation of the effectiveness and efficiency of collective redress mechanisms in the European Union. Civic Consulting & Oxford Economics

Mulheron R (2008) Reform of collective redress in England and Wales: a perspective of need. Civil Justice Council. https://www.judiciary.uk/wp-content/uploads/JCO/Documents/CJC/Publications/Other%2Bpapers/reform-of-collective-redress.pdf. Accessed 20 April 2019

Mulheron R (2014) The class action in common law legal systems: a comparative perspective. Oxford University Press, Oxford

Nagy CI (2011) A csoportos igényérvényesítés gazdaságtana és lehetőségei a magyar jogban. Jogtudományi Közlöny 66(3):163–174

Nagy CI (2012) Commitments as surrogates of civil redress in competition law: the Hungarian perspective. Eur Competition Law Rev 33(11):531–536

Nagy CI (2013) Comparative collective redress from a law and economics perspective: without risk there is no reward! Columbia J Eur Law 19(3):469–498

Neumann K-A, Magnusson LW (2011) Pour une class-action européenne dans le droit de la concurrence. Revue québécoise de droit international 24(2):149–181

Patetta G (2010) Opportunité du choix de l'opt-in/opt-out – le point de vue de l'UFC – Que choisir, l'action de collective ou action de groupe – se préparer à son introduction en droit français et en droit belge. Larcier

Silver C (2000) Class actions—representative proceedings. In: Encyclopedia of law and economics, vol 5. Edward Elgar Publishing, Cheltenham

Stuyck J (2009) Class actions in Europe? To opt-in or to opt-out, that is the question. Eur Bus Law Rev 20(4):483–505

Szalai Á (2014) Kollektív keresetek szabályozási kérdései – joggazdaságtani elemzés. Magyar Jog 61(12):706–712

Ulen TS (2011) An introduction to the law and economics of class action litigation. Eur J Law Econ 32:185–203

Ulen TS (2012) The Economics of Class Action Litigation. In: Backhaus G, Cassone A, Ramello GB (eds) The law and economics of class actions in Europe: lessons from America. Edward Elgar, Cheltenham, pp 75–98

Vanikiotisa MT (2014) Private antitrust enforcement and tentative steps toward collective redress in Europe and the United Kingdom. Fordham Int Law J 37:1639–1681

Wagner G (2009) Litigation costs and their recovery: the German experience. Civil Justice Quart 28(3):367–388
Wagner G (2011) Collective redress—categories of loss and legislative options. Law Quart Rev 127(1):55–82
Wrbka S, van Uytsel S, Siems MM (2012) Access to justice and collective actions: "Florence" and beyond. In: Wrbka S, van Uytsel S, Siems MM (eds) Collective actions: enhancing access to justice and reconciling multilayer interests?. Cambridge University Press, Cambridge, pp 1–22

Chapter 3
Major European Objections and Fears Against the Opt-Out System: Superego, Ego and Id

This chapter presents and analyses the objections against class actions and inquires why the appearance and reception of collective actions, especially the notion of "representation without authorization", have sparked furious opposition in Europe. It addresses and refutes the major arguments and fears against the opt-out system (unconstitutionality, European traditionalism, technical difficulties and abusive litigation), and inquires whether these are genuine scruples or pretexts veiling a deeper aversion against class actions. It is argued that the headspring of Europe's instinctive resistance against American class actions and the subconscious reason why it is so difficult to reconcile the "Copernican turn" of class actions with European traditionalism are the taboo of party autonomy and the state's entrenched prerogative to enforce the public interest. An inquiry into the deep layers reveals that the European reaction may be traced back to the peculiar European thinking about the relationship between the market (or private enterprise) and the public interest and the continental notion that the enforcement of the public interest is the inalienable prerogative of the state.[1]

3.1 European Objections Against Class Actions: Scruples or Pretexts?

Class actions, and in particular the notion that group members may be represented without express authorization, have been criticized from four angles. First, "representation without authorization" is claimed to be unconstitutional due to its encroachment on private autonomy and, second, to be alien to continental legal traditions. Third, the practical feasibility of class actions has been impugned with reference to technical difficulties of identification and proof. Fourth, class actions have been claimed to inflict significant social damages due to their being prone to abusive litigation (litigation boom and blackmailing potential).

---

[1]Concerning the repetitious European debate on collective actions, see Nagy (2015).

© The Author(s) 2019
C. I. Nagy, *Collective Actions in Europe*,
SpringerBriefs in Law, https://doi.org/10.1007/978-3-030-24222-0_3

3.1.1 Constitutional Concerns: Private Autonomy and Tacit Adherence

The opt-out system may raise constitutional concerns, since "representation without authorization" may impair group members' private autonomy, which consists, in this context, of the right to decide whether or not to enforce a claim and how to enforce it.[2] However, there are quite a few compelling arguments that suggest that the opt-out scheme, as far as small claims are concerned, should not be outright unconstitutional. Although the collective action may certainly be shaped in a manner that goes counter to constitutional requirements, the constitutional concerns relating to small claims are mainly an optical illusion.

European traditionalism is often wrapped up in constitutional parlance. In Germany, opt-out class actions appear to have been rejected, among others, for constitutional reasons: it has been argued that representation without authorization may raise serious constitutional concerns, e.g. it may impair the right to a hearing (Recht zum rechtlichen Gehör) and the right of disposition (Dispositionsgrundsatz).[3] While it could be argued that silence should be regarded to imply acceptance, such a legal consequence may be entailed only by proper notice and it has been highly questionable whether constructive knowledge would suffice in this regard.[4] The foregoing constitutional concerns have been taken so seriously that in 2005 the German Federal Cartel Office (Bundeskartellamt), notwithstanding the very strong policy for competition law's private enforcement, discarded the idea of opt-out collective actions apparently because it was said to restrict the right to a hearing and to violate the principle that the party is the master of his own case (right of disposition).[5]

In the context of French law, it has been consistently referred to the principle of "nul ne plaide par procureur" ("no one pleads by proxy").[6] According to this entrenched principle of French civil procedural law, for having standing, the plaintiff has to have a legitimate interest in the case and, to be legitimate, the interest must be direct and personal; as a corollary, all the persons involved in the lawsuit must be identified and represented in the procedure.[7]

It is true that mandatory representation, that is, representation without authorization not supplemented by the right to opt-out, seems to be irreconcilable with constitutional requirements. For instance, in Spain, where the judgment's res judicata effects may extend to non-litigant group members, it has been convincingly argued

---

[2]Commission Communication Towards a European Horizontal Framework for Collective Redress, COM (2013) 401 final, p. 11. See Strong (2013: 239–247) (Referring to these considerations as the plaintiff's "individual participatory right".).

[3]See Greiner (1998: 189), Fiedler (2010: 237–245), Stadler (2011: 172–173), Lange (2011: 129–171), Geiger (2015: 245–255).

[4]Stadler (2015: 569–578). For arguments that public notice in collective actions does not violate the principle of disposition, see Halfmeier (2012: 183).

[5]Bundeskartellamt (2005: 30–31).

[6]Mazen (1987: 383–384).

[7]Poisson and Fléchet (2012: 166).

that absent a specific statutory provision, the right to opt out arises from the constitutional principles of due process and access to justice.[8] However, representation without authorization supplemented with the right to opt out may merit a different treatment. It is noteworthy that this is in line with the US Supreme Court's stance that class actions based on representation without authorization meet the requirements of due process as long as members have the right to opt out.[9]

It has to be noted that a comparable set of constitutional arguments may be lined up for the introduction of collective actions.

First, in the absence of a collective litigation mechanism, numerous small claims would not get to court[10] and, hence, the collective action confers solely benefits on group members (provided they do not run the risk of being liable for the defendant's legal costs in case the group representative fails to win the action). It would be perverse to refer to the impairment of private autonomy in a case characterized by obligee inertia,[11] where the law does not ensure the claim's practical enforceability.

Second, opt-out systems embed, by definition, the right to opt out. While mandatory representation (that is, when group members are compelled to be part of the group and cannot opt out) may obviously go counter to the right to private autonomy (that is, the right to decide whether or not to sue, and how to enforce the claim), there is no "forced membership" in case of an opt-out system. Group members can leave the group without any further. The opt-out scheme merely reverses the mechanism of adherence and infers assent from silence. In principle, a group member has to submit a declaration, if he envisages being part of the action. In the opt-out system, a group member has to submit a declaration, if he does not want to be part of the action. The group member makes the decision and since experience shows that the vast majority of group members does not opt out, arguably, it is reasonable to reverse the mechanism of adherence.[12]

It has to be noted that the opt-out system is much more constitutional and preserves private autonomy much better than the EU Injunction Directive[13] covering 17 consumer protection Union acts.[14] The Directive authorizes various entities to launch proceedings for a declaratory judgment or injunction on behalf of a class of

---

[8] For a comprehensive analysis on the Spanish class action mechanism, see Mieres (2000). See also Piñeiro (2009: 61–88), Jiménez (2008), López (2001), Estagnan (2004: 9–10).

[9] *Philipps Petroleum v Shutts* 472 US 797, 813–814 (1985).

[10] Udvary (2015: 242–244).

[11] See Eisenberg and Miller (2004: 1529, 1532), Issacharoff and Miller (2009: 179, 203–206), Issacharoff and Miller (2012: 37, 60).

[12] See Eisenberg and Miller (2004: 203–206), Issacharoff and Miller (2012: 60).

[13] Directive 2009/22/EC on injunctions for the protection of consumers' interests, [2009] OJ L 110/30. See Trstenjak (2015: 689–691).

[14] See Annex I of the Directive, last amended by Directive 2019/771 on certain aspects concerning contracts for the sale of goods, amending Regulation (EU) 2017/2394 and Directive 2009/22/EC, and repealing Directive 1999/44/EC (OJ L 136, 22.5.2019, p. 28). The Annex currently lists the following 17 Union acts: Directive 85/577/EEC to protect the consumer in respect of contracts negotiated away from business premises (OJ L 372, 31.12.1985, p. 31); Directive 87/102/EEC for the approximation of the laws, regulations and administrative provisions of the Member States concerning consumer credit (OJ L 42, 12.2.1987, p. 48); Directive 89/552/EEC on the coordination of certain provisions

unidentified consumers without the need for any individual authorization or assent, and, theoretically, it does not even make it possible for group members to leave the group. This means that group members cannot opt-out even if they want to; they are stuck in the group. Still, the constitutionality of the Injunction Directive has never been questioned.

Third, it has to be noted that while the right of disposition is constitutionally protected, access to justice is equally a constitutional fundamental right. The purpose of collective litigation is to make practically unenforceable rights a reality.

Whatever the strength of these points may be, interestingly, the rigid unconstitutionality arguments have found no reflection in the constitutional case-law. This suggests that while certain limits do apply, opt-out mechanisms are not outright unconstitutional. While representation without authorization does call for a justification, it may be warranted in small-value cases, which would very likely not be brought to court anyway. The cases that can be raised from national constitutional laws, used as arguments that the opt-out scheme is irreconcilable with national constitutional requirements, can be distinguished from the enforcement of small pecuniary claims in an opt-out collective procedure. In fact, in 2014 the French Constitutional Council (Conseil constitutionnel) confirmed the recently introduced French regulatory regime, which, in certain points, has salient opt-out features.

The European Court of Human Rights (ECtHR) addressed the question of representation without authorization[15] in *Lithgow v. United Kingdom*.[16] The case emerged in the context of the UK's expropriation of a British company. To avoid the flood

---

laid down by law, regulation or administrative action in Member States concerning the pursuit of television broadcasting activities: Articles 10 to 21 (OJ L 298, 17.10.1989, p. 23); Directive 90/314/EEC on package travel, package holidays and package tours (OJ L 158, 23.6.1990, p. 59); Directive 93/13/EEC on unfair terms in consumer contracts (OJ L 95, 21.4.1993, p. 29); Directive 97/7/EC on the protection of consumers in respect of distance contracts (OJ L 144, 4.6.1997, p. 19); Directive 1999/44/EC on certain aspects of the sale of consumer goods and associated guarantees (OJ L 171, 7.7.1999, p. 12); Directive 2000/31/EC on certain legal aspects on information society services, in particular electronic commerce, in the internal market (Directive on electronic commerce) (OJ L 178, 17.7.2000, p. 1); Directive 2001/83/EC on the Community code relating to medicinal products for human use: Articles 86 to 100 (OJ L 311, 28.11.2001, p. 67); Directive 2002/65/EC concerning the distance marketing of consumer financial services (OJ L 271, 9.10.2002, p. 16); Directive 2005/29/EC concerning unfair business-to-consumer commercial practices in the internal market (OJ L 149, 11.6.2005, p. 22); Directive 2006/123/EC on services in the internal market (OJ L 376, 27.12.2006, p. 36); Directive 2008/122/EC on the protection of consumers in respect of certain aspects of timeshare, long-term holiday product, resale and exchange contracts (OJ L 33, 3.2.2009, p. 10); Directive 2013/11/EU on alternative dispute resolution for consumer disputes (OJ L 165, 18.6.2013, p. 63): Article 13; Regulation 524/2013 on online dispute resolution for consumer disputes (Regulation on consumer ODR) (OJ L 165, 18.6.2013, p. 1): Article 14; Regulation 2018/302 on addressing unjustified geo-blocking and other forms of discrimination based on customers' nationality, place of residence or place of establishment within the internal market and amending Regulations 2006/2004 and 2017/2394 and Directive 2009/22/EC (OJ L 60 I, 2.3.2018, p. 1); Directive 2019/770 on certain aspects concerning contracts for the supply of digital content and digital services (OJ L 136, 22.5.2019, p. 1).

[15]For an analysis on the ECtHR case-law, see Strong (2013: 243–245).

[16]Case no. 9006/80; 9262/81; 9263/81; 9265/81; 9266/81; 9313/81; 9405/81 *Lithgow v. United Kingdom*, 8 July 1986, [1986] 8 ECHR 329.

of individual actions, the law on nationalization provided for the appointment of a "stockholders' representative", who was to be elected by the shareholders or appointed by the government and whose power of attorney to claim compensation precluded group members' individual actions. In other words, the scheme established mandatory representation without authorization where group members were forced to join and could not opt out.

The ECtHR proceeded from the proposition, as established in *Ashingdane*,[17] that the

> right of access to the courts secured by Article 6 para. 1 (art. 6-1) is not absolute but may be subject to limitations; these are permitted by implication since the right of access 'by its very nature calls for regulation by the State, regulation which may vary in time and in place according to the needs and resources of the community and of individuals'.

The limitations may not impair the very essence of the right and need to "pursue a legitimate aim" and there needs to be "a reasonable relationship of proportionality between the means employed and the aim sought to be achieved."[18] As to the scheme at stake, the ECtHR came to the conclusion that these conditions were met. The very essence of the right to a court was not impaired,[19] because individual rights were (indirectly) safeguarded: the group representative was "appointed by and represented the interests of all" group members and individual group members could seek remedy in case the representative breached one of his duties. This conclusion was not undermined by the fact that the group members' right to control the representative was very limited and it was not the individual shareholders but their community who was entitled to exercise these rights.[20] Furthermore, the Court held that the scheme "pursued a legitimate aim, namely the desire to avoid, in the context of a large-scale nationalization measure, a multiplicity of claims and proceedings brought by individual shareholders" and there was "a reasonable relationship of proportionality between the means employed and this aim."[21]

The above jurisprudence was confirmed in *Wendenburg*.[22] Here, in the context of a procedure before the German Federal Constitutional Court (Bundesverfassungs-gericht), the ECtHR, referring to *Lithgow*, held that while "the applicants were barred from appearing individually before that court", "in proceedings involving a decision for a collective number of individuals, it is not always required or even possible that every individual concerned is heard before the court."

National constitutional courts followed a very similar line of reasoning.

In the early '90s, due to the particular historical situation, the Hungarian Constitutional Court had the chance to adjudicate cases centering around representation without authorization. In 1989, the socialist regime collapsed in Hungary and the

---

[17] Case no. 8225/78 *Ashingdane v. United Kingdom*, 28 May 1985, [1985] ECHR 8, Series A no. 93, para 57.

[18] *Lithgow*, para 194.

[19] Para 196.

[20] See Footnote 18.

[21] Para 197.

[22] Case no. 71630/01 *Wendenburg and Others v. Germany*, 6 February 2003, [2003-II] ECHR 353.

country adopted a new constitution,[23] while the laws adopted beforehand persisted. Although the parliament tried to weed Hungarian law of the provisions that were not reconcilable with a constitutional democracy, some reminiscences remained and had to be quashed by the Constitutional Court itself. One of these was the rules of socialist law that conferred mandatory representation without authorization on the attorney general and trade unions. These entities could launch civil proceedings even against the obligee's will. These laws had a very peculiar feature: the right of representation of these entities was general and mandatory, that is, they not only lacked the party's authorization, but the represented person could not opt out and terminate his own action. These rules were struck down by the Constitutional Court. However, the court also established that, if justified, "representation without authorization" can be constitutional. Albeit that these cases involved no class actions, they provide clear guidance also as to the opt-out principle's constitutionality.

In *Case 8/1990 (IV.23.) AB*, the Hungarian Constitutional Court dealt with trade unions' right to represent an employee without authorization. The constitutional concerns were entailed by the trade union's "mandatory power of attorney" and not by a "presumed power of attorney." The legislation did not prevent trade unions from exercising the right of representation against the employee's will, which were authorized to intervene also in matters where the employee was not a member of the trade union. The Constitutional Court suggested that the legislator may maintain the trade union's right of representation in relation to its own members.

In *Case 1/1994. (I.7.) AB*, the Constitutional Court dealt with the attorney general's power to act on behalf of private parties. The Court held that party autonomy (right of disposition) embraces both the liberty to act and the liberty not to act; the attorney general's all-pervasive power to sue and appeal without the party's express assent restricts the party's constitutional rights and needs to be examined whether this restriction is necessary and proportionate. In this case, the Constitutional Court came to the conclusion that there were no constitutionally acceptable legitimate ends justifying the attorney general's blanket power to act on behalf of the party. Here again, the most important source of concern was the attorney general's "mandatory power of attorney", which—if warranted by an important national or economic interest—could be exercised also against the party's will. At the same time, the Constitutional Court did not question the attorney general's power to sue in cases where the obligee was not able to protect his rights. Quite the contrary, the Court held that in such cases representation without authorization is considered an inevitable restriction of party autonomy (right of disposition) and

> the protection of the subjective rights of the party who is unable to enforce or protect his rights is the constitutional obligation of the state. Accordingly, the state has to ensure that in such cases one of its organs acts for the sake of protecting the rights of the individual.

---

[23]Technically, it amended the old constitution comprehensively. However, in essence, the amendment, in fact, created a new constitution.

In sum, the case-law of the Hungarian Constitutional Court suggests that representation without authorization may meet the constitutional requirements, if it is justified by a legitimate end. Both the absence of a "mandatory power of attorney" and the party's right to opt out point towards compliance with the constitutional requirements. While the above cases give no guidance as to whether public notice is sufficient or group members need to be informed individually about the collective action and the right to opt out, they indicate that if the party is unable to protect his rights, the state is even obliged to intervene.

The French Constitutional Council (Conseil Constitutionnel) examined the question of representation without authorization[24] first in 1989 in the context of trade unions' right to launch proceedings on behalf of their members, and recently it scrutinized the de facto opt-out mechanism introduced by the French legislator in 2014.

The matter concerning group actions initiated by a trade union on behalf of its members became famous in the European scholarship on class actions and had been referred to as an authority to justify the unconstitutionality of the opt-out system. Not surprisingly, this case centered around the issue of proper notice, which was considered to be an essential requirement against representation without authorization.

Here, the French Constitutional Council held that the employee is to be "afforded the opportunity to give his assent with full knowledge of the facts and that he remained free to conduct personally the defense of his interests" and he shall have the opportunity to opt out from the procedure. Furthermore, "the employee concerned must be informed by registered letter with a form of acknowledgement of receipt in order that he may, if he desires so, object to the trade union's initiative." This ruling was interpreted by many as excluding the possibility of an opt-out system as such schemes secure no actual knowledge.[25]

Although this question lost much of its significance, as the 1989 decision, whatever its proper construction may be, seems to have been jumped by the 2014 decision analyzed below, it has to be noted that, arguably, the fact pattern addressed by the 1989 decision can be distinguished from opt-out systems in small claim procedures. The former dealt with a law that authorized trade unions to launch any action (toutes actions) on behalf of the employee, including claims of unfair dismissal.[26] Pecuniary small claims can be clearly distinguished from employment law claims at large, especially unfair dismissal matters: the latter normally involve higher stakes, higher monetary value and may lead to the employee's readmission (which entails personal consequences). Furthermore, the French Constitutional Council did not hold that representation without authorization or inference of the right of representation from the employee's silence would be unconstitutional. Quite the contrary, it held

---

[24] In relation to French constitutional considerations, see Poisson and Fléchet (2012: 65–166).

[25] Dec. Cons. Const. N°89-257 DC, July 25th 1989. Reproduced in Magnier and Alleweldt (2008: 2).

[26] Id. at para 25.

that if the employee fails to object to the trade union's procedure, he can be regarded as adhering to it.[27] The French Constitutional Council treated this case rather as an issue of notice: the employee has to be informed by registered mail and actual notice has to be ensured.[28] Accordingly, the requirement established by the French Constitutional Council concerning opt-out regimes was proper notice. It has to be taken into consideration that, as noted above, the French statute's opt-out scheme covered the whole spectrum of employment claims and the constitutional requirements concerning the means of notice may be less stringent in case of small-value pecuniary claims.

In 2014, France adopted collective action rules that remained within the limits set up by the decision of 1989. Although under the rules of 2014, the group representative may launch a collective action without the express authorization of group members, the final judgment, in essence, will extend only to those who expressly accept the award; at this stage, tacit adherence is not sufficient. This regime passed the test of constitutionality. It seems that it was decisive for the French Constitutional Council that the res judicata effects cover solely those group members who received compensation at the end of the procedure.[29] Apparently, the circumstance that only benefits accrue to group members and that the judgment's res judicata effects cover only those group members who assented to it (since compensation can be paid only if the group member accepts the final judgment), were sufficient to satisfy the constitutional concerns.

All in all, although opt-out collective actions do raise constitutional issues in some EU Member States, the above arguments and case-law suggest that they are far from irreconcilable with the constitutional traditions common to the European Union's Member States.

3.1.2 Opt-Out Collective Actions Are Alien to Continental Legal Traditions

This statement is, in fact, not true. It may have been true some decades ago, however, in the last couple of decades Europe has seen the appearance of collective action laws in a number of Member States that enable the enforcement of pecuniary claims in an opt-out system (as will be discussed below). Furthermore, EU law itself contains a very important and popular opt-out mechanism that permits representation without authorization (EU Injunction Directive).

---

[27]Id. at paras 25–26.

[28]Id. at para 26.

[29]Decision 2014-690 of 13 March 2014 (Le 14 novembre 2014, JORF n°0065 du 18 mars 2014, Texte n°2, Décision n° 2014-690 DC du 13 mars 2014), paras 10 and 16.

The Injunction Directive covers 17 consumer protection Union acts[30] and empowers various entities to launch proceedings for a declaratory judgment or injunction on behalf of a class of unidentified consumers, without any need for individual authorization or assent. The proposition that judgments rendered in collective actions for an injunction may and shall have legal effects on all interested consumers was confirmed by the CJEU in Case C-472/10 *Nemzeti Fogyasztóvédelmi Hatóság v Invitel Távközlési Zrt.*[31] The case dealt with Article 7 of the Unfair Terms Directive,[32] which enshrines a similar collective action for injunction. The ruling may be extrapolated to all collective actions coming under the Injunction Directive.

> "[T]he national courts are required (…) to draw all the consequences provided for by national law in order to ensure that consumers who have concluded a contract to which those GBC [general business conditions] apply will not be bound by that term. (…) [The Directive] does not preclude the declaration of invalidity of an unfair term included in the GBC of consumer contracts in an action for an injunction (…) from producing, in accordance with that legislation, effects with regard to all consumers who concluded with the seller or supplier concerned a contract to which the same GBC apply, including with regard to those consumers who were not party to the injunction proceedings; *where the unfair nature of a term in the GBC has been acknowledged in such proceedings, national courts are required*, of their own motion, and also with regard to the future, *to take such action* thereon as is provided for by national law *in order to ensure that consumers who have concluded a contract with the seller or supplier to which those GBC apply will not be bound by that term.*"[33]

What is more, the procedure provided for by the Injunction Directive is, literally speaking, not an opt-out scheme (in fact, it is "worse"), since it does not make it possible for group members to leave the group. That is, group members cannot opt out even if they want to—they are stuck in the group. Although pecuniary claims cannot be enforced by means of this mechanism, from the perspective of legal tradition this should make no difference, since both pecuniary and non-pecuniary claims are, legally speaking, claims. It seems that there is no legitimate reason to accept the opt-out system for declaratory judgments and injunctions and to pronounce this an alien conception in relation to pecuniary claims.

Although the opt-out system does qualify as a minority position in Europe, it is far from being unknown. Currently, in the European Union there are 10 Member States where it is possible to enforce pecuniary claims in an opt-out system: Bulgaria,[34]

---

[30]See Annex I of the Directive, last amended by Directive 2019/771 on certain aspects concerning contracts for the sale of goods, amending Regulation (EU) 2017/2394 and Directive 2009/22/EC, and repealing Directive 1999/44/EC (OJ L 136, 22.5.2019, p. 28).

[31]ECLI:EU:C:2012:242.

[32]Directive 93/13/EEC on unfair terms in consumer contracts (OJ L 95, 21.4.1993, p. 29).

[33]Paras 43–44 (emphasis added).

[34]Chapter 33, Sections 379–388 of the Bulgarian Code of Civil Procedure, for an English version of the statutory text, see https://kenarova.com/law/Code%20of%20Civil%20Procedure.pdf. Accessed 20 April 2019. See Katzarsky and Georgiev (2012: 64).

Belgium,[35] Denmark,[36] France, Greece,[37] Hungary,[38] Portugal,[39] Slovenia,[40] Spain[41] and the United Kingdom.[42] As illustrated above, although French law adopted a unique pattern, which formally retained the requirement of opt-in, the French system can be characterized as a de facto opt-out system. This means that approximately one-third of the Member States has an opt-out system in place.[43]

Finally, it appears to be perverse to use tradition as a blocking argument when drafting a new scheme. It hardly seems to be reasonable to reject a new regulatory solution simply on the basis that it is new. The opt-out scheme is, indeed, a novel regulatory solution in continental Europe, however, it can be judged only after a full-blown analysis, taking into account its merits and drawbacks. It would be truly perverse to say, in the course of searching for the regulatory solution to be adopted, that a new regulatory concept should not be adopted simply because it is new and not part of the law (the law which is considered for reform).

---

[35] The Belgian system leaves it to the judge to decide whether the action should be conducted in the opt-in or the opt-out scheme. Law Inserting Title 2 on "Collective Compensation Action" in Book XVII "Special Jurisdictional Procedures" of the Code of Economic Law, 28 March 2014, Moniteur Belge (M.B.) (Official Gazette of Belgium (29 March 2014) (Loi portant insertion d'un titre 2 «De l'action en réparation collective» au livre XVII «Procédures juridictionnelles particulières» du Code de droit économique et portant insertion des définitions propres au livre XVII dans le livre 1er du Code de droit économique).

[36] In Denmark, it is up to the court to decide whether the action has to be conducted in the opt-in or the opt-out system. Sections 254a–254e of the Administration of Justice Act (Lov om rettens pleje). The rules on collective actions were inserted through Act no. 181 of 28 February 2007. This is very similar to the Norvegian system where it is up to the court to decide whether the proceedings have to be carried out in the opt-in or the opt-out system. Chapter 35 of Act of 17 June 2005 no. 90 relating to mediation and procedure in civil disputes (The Dispute Act) (Lov om mekling og rettergang i sivile tvister (tvisteloven)). See Kiurunen and Lindström (2012: 234).

[37] Articles 10(16)-(29) of Law 2251/1994 on Consumers' Protection. For an English translation, see https://www.eccgreece.gr/wp-content/uploads/2015/07/N2251-1994-enc2007-en1.pdf.

[38] Section 92 of Hungarian Competition Act (1996. évi LVII. törvény a tisztességtelen piaci magatartás és a versenykorlátozás tilalmáról); Sections 38-38/A of Hungarian Consumer Protection Act (Act CLV of 1997) (1997. évi CLV. törvény a fogyasztóvédelemről).

[39] Act 83/95, of 31 August, on Procedural Participation and Popular Action (Lei n.o 83/95, de 31 de Agosto, Direito de Participação Procedimental e de Acção Popular), as revised by Decree-Law 214-G/2015, of 2 October.

[40] Law on Collective Actions (Zakon o kolektivnih tožbah—ZkolT), Official Journal of the Republic of Slovenia No. 55/2017.

[41] Section 11 of Spanish Code on Civil Procedure (Ley 1/2000, de 7 de enero, de Enjuiciamiento Civil).

[42] Part 19.6 (Representative parties with same interest) of Civil Procedure Rules (CPR). Andrews (2001: 251–252), Sherman (2002: 401–432). In the mechanism recently introduced in competition law, the Competition Appeal Tribunal decides, in a collective proceedings order, whether the procedure has to be carried out in the opt-in or the opt-out system, Sections 47A–49E of Competition Act 1998, inserted by Part 1 of Schedule 8 of the Consumer Rights Act 2015. See Waller (2015: 21–24).

[43] Nagy (2010: 138–143).

The innovation of today is the tradition of tomorrow. Although its roots can be traced back to equity,[44] the institution of class action was inserted into US federal procedural law only in 1938. This regime was profoundly revised in 1966 and subjected to some minor changes in 2003.[45] It can be established that the US system of class action was finalized in 1966, since it was the 1966 reform that made the wide-spread use of class actions possible.[46] Today, this regulation is regarded as the "American tradition", contrary to the continental tradition.

The classical litigation system proceeds from the assumption that the parties to the action are equal both in terms of money and capacity, have unlimited free time and resources to present their case. The reality of the 21st century is, however, not this. The age of masses is characterized by standardized contracts and standardized cases. The projection of the mass economy has already appeared in substantive law: the regime on unfair terms in standardized consumer contracts is based on the recognition of the fact that in the mass economy individual enterprises face masses. Collective actions recognize this in procedural law. "[I]ndividually tailored law-suits for consumers are often as much an anachronism as the concept that all cars that are put on the market should be handcrafted (...). [E]conomies of scale now dictate mass redress procedures for consumers prejudiced by a common legal wrong."[47]

3.1.3 It Is Very Difficult to Identify the Members of the Group and to Prove Group Membership

It is a frequent argument against class actions that in opt-out systems group members do not (or normally do not) get their money and the benefits of opt-out actions (that is, the moneys awarded) go to group representatives. The Commission's Recommendation on Collective Redress contends that "an 'opt-out' system may not be consistent with the central aim of collective redress, which is to obtain compensation for harm suffered, since such persons are not identified, and *so the award will not be distributed to them.*"[48]

The above assertion is based on a fatal misunderstanding. Just as opt-in systems, opt-out collective action mechanisms aim to provide recovery to group members and, as a general rule, the award is normally distributed to group members and they really

---

[44]*Montgomery Ward & Co. v Langer*, 168 F2d 182, 187 (1948); Yeazell (1987), Eizenga and Davis (2011: 8–9).

[45]Dumain (2005: 221–248) and Edward (2002: 432–440).

[46]See e.g. Pace (2008: 2), Eizenga and Davis (2011: 16), Coffee (2017: 1896), Hensler (2017: 966) (Referring to 1966 as the year of birth of the US class action.).

[47]Trebilcock (1976: 270).

[48]Commission Recommendation of 11 June 2013 on common principles for injunctive and compensatory collective redress mechanisms in the Member States concerning violations of rights granted under Union Law, p. 12. (emphasis added).

receive the money.[49] Although in certain systems "fluid recovery" or "cy pres" is available,[50] this does not have to be necessarily adopted along with the introduction of collective actions (though it is advisable).

Obviously, it is much simpler to allot the award in an opt-in system, since here group members are identified by coming forward to join the action. However, the award can be distributed to group members also in the opt-out system, if group members are identifiable. It is a regulatory choice whether the availability of collective actions should be limited to cases where group members are clearly identifiable and what degree of "identifiability" should be required. However, in numerous cases, the court judgment can define the group properly: by way of example, the subscribers of a dominant cable television company between 1 January and 31 December 2018; or those persons who had to pay a higher vehicle registration tax, which proved to be contrary to the rules of the internal market; or those EU citizens who had to pay a discriminatory tuition fee for the academic year of 2018–2019. Such a definition would make group members easily identifiable.

Although it is true that in certain cases it is difficult or even impossible to create a definition for identifying group members, this can be accomplished in numerous other cases. As a legislative option, identifiability could be made a pre-requisite of collective litigation. However, it would be perverse to argue that since the opt-out scheme would not work in certain cases, due to the lack of identifiability, it should be abandoned also in cases where it could work.

Contrary to the Recommendation's assertion, in case of opt-out collective actions, the biggest trouble is not that group members are not identified—since, as noted, identifiability can be made a pre-requisite of the collective action. An important problem is that in certain cases group members are legally identifiable but proof of group membership may face serious practical hurdles. For instance, assume that taxi drivers fix prices, thus overcharging customers.[51] Although the violation of antitrust law is proven and group members are legally identifiable, it is assumed that the vast majority of the victims would not be able to prove their membership, since they usually do not keep the receipts.

Nonetheless, even if group members cannot turn the award into cash, this does not necessarily entail that their share is paid out by the defendant (although it is easy

---

[49] As regards claims administration, see Kinsella and Wheatman (2010: 273–274), Kinsella and Wheatman (2012: 338–348).

[50] See Alexander (2000: 16), Foer (2012: 349–364) ("The normal remedies in a private antitrust case are a combination of injunctions and treble damages that are paid to the victim or victims of the anticompetitive activity. When an aggregate amount of damages is established, the primary objective is to distribute the damages to those who were injured. In antitrust class action litigation, however, it is often impossible or impracticable to compensate all victims. Administrative concerns may work against payments to individual plaintiffs, as in the case of an extremely large class where the fund is not sufficient to justify the transaction costs of distribution to individual claimants. Consequently, in some cases, there is money left over in the form of unclaimed funds. In such cases, courts sometimes employ the doctrine of 'cy pres' to put the unclaimed funds to 'the next best use,' which may include awarding funds to public interest organizations or charities for purposes related to the case.").

[51] Alexander (2000: 16).

to argue that the wrongdoer should not keep the windfall of his mischief). Collective litigation does not necessarily imply collective enforcement. Although it is submitted that collective action mechanisms should encompass collective enforcement, there is no indication in the Recommendation that the proposed collective mechanism would extend to enforcement as well. In fact, it is a major shortcoming of most European schemes that they ignore that the purpose of the action, as far as pecuniary claims are concerned, is not a judgment but money.

Finally, it is submitted that while it is not inevitable that the share of non-identifiable group members is paid out to the group representative, it would be reasonable to oblige wrongdoers to pay compensation also for legally or practically non-identifiable group members. The law cannot leave the enrichment earned through an illegal conduct with the wrongdoer. From a social perspective, it appears to be more reasonable to give a windfall to the group representative than to leave an illegal enrichment with the wrongdoer (it is to be noted that this would not even amount to a windfall, taking into account that the group representative does invest a lot in the claim's enforcement). It is tempting to argue that this non-distributable money should be spent on a public interest purpose, like funding collective actions.

It is worthy of note that an effective collective action mechanism yields the highest benefits not when it is used but when it is not; collective actions may make practically unavailable civil recovery a reality. While in the absence of collective action several rules and rights established by the law are regarded as practically non-existent (and practically unenforceable), effective collective litigation makes the violation of these rules extremely risky and prompts enterprises to respect them.

3.1.4 Opt-Out Collective Actions Would Lead to a Litigation Boom and Would Create a Black-Mailing Potential for Group Representatives

Perhaps the most popular misunderstanding in respect of opt-out collective actions is that, similarly to US law, it would lead to a litigation boom and would enable group representatives, who aggregate a mass of claims, to blackmail defendants and to wring illegitimate settlements from them.[52] These fears are completely unfounded.

There is no causality between the opt-out system and the alleged American litigation boom and blackmailing potential. In the US, the high number of class actions and the defendants' inclination to settle are not due to the opt-out rule but to the regulatory and social environment that surrounds this model.[53] Namely, US law contains a set of rules that are unrelated to class actions but catalyze their operation. By way of example, under US law, generous punitive damages are available and certain statutes

---

[52]See e.g. Hodges (2008: 131–132).

[53]For a detailed presentation of the statistical data, see Nagy (2013: 490–495).

provide for treble damages[54]; the "American rule" on attorney's fees does not follow the "loser pays" principle (that is, the parties pay their attorney irrespective of the action's outcome); certain statutes (for example the Sherman Act, the Magnuson-Moss Warranty Act) provide for one-way cost-shifting: if the claimant wins, he is entitled to compensation for his reasonable attorney's fees but this does not work the other way around; statistics demonstrate that the American society is much more litigious than the European[55]; the operation of litigators is normally based on contingency fees and law firms work according to an entrepreneurial model,[56] where the law-firm invests money and working hours in the action, thus, in exchange for an appropriate risk premium, it takes over the risks of litigation from the parties; finally, jury trials and extensive pre-trial discovery smooth things down for the plaintiff and reinforce these factors. Taking this into account, it is easy to see that the alleged litigation boom and black-mailing potential (provided they exist) are as much peculiar to individual actions as to class actions. These are general features of the US system and not a specific characteristic of the class action.

The above is reinforced by practical experiments. The opt-out system is available in 10 EU Member States and none of these saw a "litigation boom" (not even a "litigation pop").[57] In a continental legal and social environment, the opt-out system operates in a completely different manner than in the US. The experiences in Australia[58] and Canada[59] are also informative. In these countries, the opt-out class action was introduced (at federal and state level) and while it has provided effective remedy to group members,[60] no litigation boom occurred.[61] Finally, it should not be disregarded that Europe is not the only region of the world where collective actions had to be accommodated to a civil-law environment: this happened in a number of Latin-American countries.[62]

---

[54]*BMW of North America, Inc. v. Gore*, 517 US 559, 116 S.Ct. 1589 (1996); *Cooper Indus. v. Leatherman Tool*, 532 US 424, 432, 121 S.Ct. 1678, 1683 (2001).

[55]See Gryphon (2011: 567), Rodger (2011).

[56]Alexander (2000: 12). Although attorney commercials are prohibited or restricted in several EU Member States, recently these prohibitions were eliminated or softened in quite of few legal systems. See Commission Report on Competition in Professional Services, COM/2004/83 finalm p. 14; Stephen and Love (2000: 987–1017).

[57]Nagy (2013: 490–493).

[58]In Australia, the institution of collective action was introduced into federal law in 1992. Federal Court of Australia Amendment Act 1991 (No. 181 of 1991). See Clark and Harris (2001: 289–320).

[59]Several provinces of Canada introduced the institution of collective action, such as British Columbia, Class Proceeding Act 1995, S.B.C. ch 21 (1995); Ontario, Class Proceeding Act 1992, S.O. ch 6 (1992); Quebec, Quebec Civil Code, Book IX.; Newfoundland & Labrador, Class Actions Act, S.N.L., ch. C-18.1 (2001) (Newfoundland & Labrador); Saskatchewan, The Class Actions Act, S.S., ch. C-12.01 (2001) (Saskatchewan). The institution of class action is also part of the Federal Court Rules. Federal Court Rules, Part 5.1, Sections 334.1-39.

[60]For an empirical analysis on the compensation forced out by class actions in Canada, see Piché (2018).

[61]For a detailed presentation of the statistical data, see Nagy (2013: 493–495). For a comparative analysis of Australia, Canada (Ontario and British Columbia) and the US, see Mulheron (2014).

[62]See Gidi (2003: 311–408), Gidi (2012: 901–940).

According to European fears, the group representative can create an aggregate of claims through bunching a vast number of demands and can force out an unfair settlement with the defendant even in frivolous cases.[63] However, this blackmailing potential is an illusion. A group representative enforcing a €1 billion claim-aggregate has exactly the same blackmailing potential as the representative of a €1 billion individual claim. If European eyes see a black-mailing potential in the US system, this is not due to the US class action but to those principles and rules of general application which characterize the US system at large. For instance, because of the "American rule" on attorney's fees, for the defendant, a settlement is a more attractive alternative, even if the plaintiff's case is weak, since the defendant has to bear the attorney's fees, even if he wins the case and the plaintiff's claim proves to be frivolous. If the defendant enters a settlement, he can save the attorney's fees. Furthermore, punitive damages and treble damages may multiply the action's expected costs.

Assume that the legal costs attached to the action are € 200,000–200,000 for the plaintiff and the defendant, respectively; they have to bear these expenses irrespective of the outcome of the action. The claim's value is € 1,000,000 and the plaintiff has a very weak case with a minuscule 10% chance to win. The claimant sues for the breach of antitrust rules, thus, under the Sherman Act, he is entitled to treble damages; furthermore, as an exception to the general "American rule", he can claim reimbursement for his reasonable attorney's fees in case he wins (that is, there is one-way cost-shifting).[64]

Accordingly, (if disregarding court fees, inflation and the procedure's length) a rational plaintiff would decide whether to sue on the basis of the following calculation. On the expected costs side, the expenses run to € 200,000. The expected income is the product of the claim's value, the reimbursement for legal costs and the chance of success: € 320,000 = (€ 1,000,000 × 3 + € 200,000) × 10%. As a corollary, the balance of the law-suit is positive: € 320,000 − € 200,000 = € 120,000, so it is rational for the plaintiff to sue.

The defendant, on the expenses side, also faces attorney's fees in value of € 200,000 (which are not recoverable) and there is 10% chance that he will have to pay 3 × € 1,000,000 as damages and € 200,000 as reimbursement for the plaintiff's reasonable attorney's fees: (€ 1,000,000 × 3 + € 200,000) × 10% + € 200,000 = € 520,000. At the same time, he cannot expect any income, since even if he wins, the only "return" is that he does not have to pay damages (the expected income is € 0). Accordingly, the defendant's balance is negative (€ −520,000 = € −200,000 + € −320,000). The defendant's expected loss attached to the action is very significant in comparison to the claim's value, although he has 90% chance to win.

Under such circumstances, the parties will endeavor to reach a settlement, where the plaintiff does not accept less than € 120,000 and the defendant is not willing to pay more than € 520,000. The precise amount will depend on the parties' bargaining

---

[63] Commission Communication Towards a European Horizontal Framework for Collective Redress, COM(2013) 401 final, pp. 7–8.

[64] 15 USC. § 15.

skills. It is noteworthy that in the above case it is rational for the defendant to pay a sum that is higher than 50% of the claim's value, while the plaintiff has merely 10% chance to win.

If we put the above case in a continental legal environment, it would not be rational for the plaintiff to sue due to the low chance of success. For the plaintiff, the action's expected income is € 100,000 (€ 1,000,000 × 10%), while there is 90% chance that he will have to bear both his and the winning defendant's legal costs (€ 400,000 × 90% = € 360,000). Accordingly, the plaintiff's balance is negative (€ 100,000 − € 360,000 = € −260,000); this is due to the lack of treble damages and to the European approach on legal costs (two-way cost shifting).

3.2 The Headspring of European Taboos and Traditionalism: Party Autonomy and the State's Prerogative to Enforce the Public Interest

Interestingly, for the most part, the European resistance against class actions has been, ostensibly, rather dogmatic and, sadly, less based on public policy and "social engineering" considerations.[65] The opt-out principle puts the traditional European conception of civil procedure upside-down. While a civil procedure (in most parts of the world) centers around the claims pursued, the "Copernican turn" of class actions is that, so as to secure effective enforcement, they put the procedure in the center and organize the claims around it.[66] Nonetheless, this dogmatic rigidity is backed by the entrenched social concept that private litigation may have no public policy function, as this comes under the prerogative of the state. Class actions interfere with this ontological principle of civil procedure in Europe. Arguably, the public policy aversion against class actions got a specious constitutional label: party autonomy.

In the European tradition (as in most civil justice systems), civil procedure centers around the claims pursued and in the standard paradigm the procedure is a negligible inconvenience in comparison to the claim itself. This paradigm[67] proceeds from the sample situation where both parties are equal in rank and fortune and have unlimited time and resources to litigate and, either for this reason or because of the value of the claim, they do not grudge the money for financing the law-suit. On the other hand, in class actions, claims center around the procedure: the primary consideration is feasibility and effectiveness and individual claims are expected to adapt themselves

---

[65]Concerning the use of civil litigation to pursue public policy goals, see Karlsgodt (2012: 49).

[66]Cf. Azar-Baud (2012: 14) (In collective proceedings one needs to sacrifice certain procedural principles in order to enable access to justice.).

[67]Cf. Mazen (1987: 373) ("La procédure civile est en Europe largement imprégnée par un individualisme ancestral et se trouve, de ce fait, souvent inadaptée à une société de consommation marquée par l'ampleur des rapports de groupe et par la multiplication des contrats portant sur de faibles montants.").

to this (of course, without losing the right to individual litigation). The "Copernican turn" of class actions is that, instead of the claim, they focus on the procedure.

The European dogmatic criticism has veiled a very strong subconscious repulsion against opt-out class actions: it seems that European legal thinking feels aversion to private litigation's having a public policy role (or even side-effect) and considers the latter to be the exclusive prerogative of the state, although collective actions are closely supervised and controlled by the court, from the opening of the procedure to the approval of a settlement and adoption of the final judgment.[68] This is in sharp contrast with the American conception of the relationship between public policy and civil litigation, which stands out markedly in case of class actions.[69] The 1966 introduction of opt-out collective actions was inspired by the idea that collective litigation on behalf of large groups of people could effectively supplement the government's regulatory and enforcement efforts, especially in case of small claims which would not get to court anyway.[70] Furthermore, "[c]ivil rights cases and other suits seeking social change or to implement institutional reform were, in many ways, the quintessential type of class action envisioned at the time of the 1966 amendments."[71]

It is very telling that the resistance of European dogmatism was less strong in cases where the opt-out principle's social impact was limited or even insignificant. This may suggest that the apprehension about the privatization of a parcel of public policy was an unspoken argument against class actions. For instance, Directive 2009/22/EC, which consolidated Directive 98/27/EC and its amendments, empowers administrative agencies and consumer organizations to institute proceedings in an opt-out system for the infringement of the EU's consumer protection rules. Currently, Directive 2009/22/EC lists 17 EU consumer protection Union acts that are strengthened by the possibility of collective action. However, the Directive is limited to claims for injunction and declaratory judgment[72]; that is, this opt-out mechanism can be used to protect consumer rights short of monetary remedies.[73] Accordingly, the question emerges: if the opt-out system, notwithstanding the dogmatic aversion, may be acceptable as to non-monetary civil remedies, why should it not be acceptable as to monetary remedies? The answer might be that class actions are perceived to be a tool of privatizing public policy and this seems to be clearly alien to European civil-law. Absent the very special US regulatory environment (punitive damages, American rule on attorney's fees, contingency fees, pre-trial discovery etc.), in Europe class

---

[68] See Falla (2014).

[69] Cf. *Zenith Radio Corp. v. Hazeltine Research, Inc.*, 395 U. S. 100, 395 U. S. 130–131 (1969) ("[T]he purpose of giving private parties treble damage and injunctive remedies was not merely to provide private relief, but was to serve as well the high purpose of enforcing the antitrust laws."); Rathod and Vaheesan (2016: 308).

[70] See Kalven and Rosenfield (1941: 684).

[71] Pace (2008).

[72] Article 7 provides that Member States are free to give these organizations "more extensive rights to bring action at national level."

[73] See Koch (2001: 363).

actions are simply not susceptible of playing a policy role similar or even compara-ble to that played on the other side of the Atlantic. Still, it seems that the European reception has be impregnated by this fear.

The above traditionalist considerations emerged under various constitutional labels. These may be boiled down to the concept of party autonomy, which proved to be one of the most devastating arguments against opt-out class actions. Perversely, party autonomy is treated as a value in itself and is fiercely protected even against the right-holders' interests and presumed will: it is used as an argument against rep-resentation without authorization even in cases where it is empirically proven that virtually none of the group members would be inclined to make use of this autonomy and group members would only benefit from the class action. Obviously, it would be difficult to argue that party autonomy is more deeply rooted in Europe than in the United States. Instead, it seems that the stifling impact of this legal principle is not due to the comparatively higher significance attributed to it in Europe but to a strange blend of European dogmatism and the aversion against private litigation's public policy role.

According to the conservative thinking, party autonomy (the right of disposi-tion) embraces the liberty to decide whether or not to enforce a claim, and implies that if someone decides to enforce it, he should be the master of his own case.[74] While citizens are free to waive some of their rights stemming from this liberty or to authorize others to exercise their rights, this has to be based on actual intent instead of constructive acceptance or presumed authorization. This argument is wrapped up in traditionalism (the opt-out principle is irreconcilable with the Euro-pean legal tradition) and constitutionalism (representation without authorization is unconstitutional).

However, none of these arguments are sweeping (at least not as much as they were two decades ago). First, the European tradition has changed: currently there are 10 Member States which have an opt-out scheme; not to mention that as to non-monetary relief, due to Directive 2009/22/EC, Member States have a general obligation to provide for an opt-out mechanism in consumer matters. It would be difficult to argue that something that is practiced in 10 Member States and is demanded in respect of non-monetary claims is alien to the European tradition and thinking. Second, while the concept of representation without authorization has, at times, met fierce criticism, in fact, the constitutional requirements proved to be manageable when they were actually tested (see Sect. 3.1.1).

3.3   Summary

In the European scholarly discourse, resistance against US class actions has been predominantly dogmatic (constitutional doctrine of party autonomy) but, subcon-sciously, backed by the settled European thinking that the enforcement of public policy is the inalienable prerogative of the state and may not be privatized. Indeed,

---

[74]Cf. Buxbaum (2014: 589–590).

the "Copernican turn" of opt-out collective litigation interferes with the ontological principles of European civil procedure: while a civil procedure traditionally centers around the claim, in the US class action claims center around the procedure.

European traditionalism has been often wrapped up in constitutional parlance, but the arguments against class actions' constitutional conformity have found no reflection in the constitutional case-law. This suggests that while certain limits do apply, opt-out mechanisms are not outright unconstitutional and they may be constitutionally warranted in small value cases, which would very likely not be brought to court anyway.

The scholarship is replete with pieces supporting the introduction of the opt-out model in Europe and, disregarding the misconceived references to legal tradition and the phobia of foreign legal solutions, one can rarely find any analysis that would convincingly demonstrate that opt-out collective actions would lead to a litigation boom, settlements forced out by black-mailing and abuses.

The alleged repercussions of opt-out collective litigation in the US do not occur when this regulatory mechanism is transplanted to a European environment. Legal rules do not operate in a vacuum but are part of a legal, social, cultural and economic environment. US law contains a large set of institutions that catalyze the operation of the opt-out class action. In Europe, failing this catalyzing environment, the alleged excesses of the US practice are not to be expected. This conclusion is underpinned by the limited European empirical evidence on opt-out collective actions and by the examples of foreign legal systems that are comparable to the European regulatory environment and have adopted US-style class action schemes (Australia, Canada, Latin America).

As demonstrated above, in class action cases group representatives have the very same black-mailing potential (if any) as the plaintiff in an individual action. The US litigation landscape is shaped by legal institutions like punitive and treble damages, the "American rule" on attorney's fees and one-way-cost shifting in certain cases, contingency fees, entrepreneurial law firms and litigious attitudes. This regulatory and social environment, which is responsible for what many Europeans attribute to class actions, is completely missing in Europe.

It seems that the European debate could not fully avoid the "ice-cream-shark-attacks" fallacy (also known as the "ice-cream-murder" fallacy). Studies show that the consumption of ice cream and shark attacks are positively correlated: the more ice cream is sold, the more shark attacks occur; and vice versa, the less ice cream is consumed, the less people are attacked by sharks. Is there correlation between the two? Yes, of course. Would it be reasonable to draw the conclusion that there is causation and advise people not to eat ice-cream to avoid shark attacks? Would abstention from ice-cream make our lives safer? No, of course, it would not. Both ice cream consumption and shark attacks increase in the summertime, when the number of people swimming in the seas and oceans is uncomparably higher than during winter, hence, the chances of shark attacks are obviously higher. Correlation does not mean causation. The alleged link between the US class action and certain abusive practices is nothing more but an optical illusion. A closer look at the perceived relationship confirms that there is not causation between the two, it is simple correlation.

References

Alexander JC (2000) An introduction to class action procedure in the United States. Paper presented at "Debates over group litigation in comparative perspective", Geneva, 21–22 July 2000. http://law.duke.edu/grouplit/papers/classactionalexander.pdf. Accessed 20 April 2019

Andrews N (2001) Multi-party proceedings in England: representative and group actions. Duke J Compar Int Law 11(2):249–267

Azar-Baud MJ (2012) La nature juridique des actions collectives en droit de la consommation. Revue européenne de droit de la consommation 1:3–28

Bundeskartellamt (2005) Diskussionspapier: Private Kartellrechtsdurchsetzung – Stand, Probleme, Perspektiven. http://www.bundeskartellamt.de/SharedDocs/Publikation/DE/Diskussions_Hintergrundpapier/Bundeskartellamt%20-%20Private%20Kartellrechtsdurchsetzung.html?nn=3590858. Accessed on 20 April 2019

Buxbaum HL (2014) Class actions, conflict and the global economy. Ind J Global Legal Stud 21(2):585–597

Clark SS, Harris C (2001) Multi-plaintiff litigation in Australia: a comparative perspective. Duke J Compar Int Law 11(2):289–320

Coffee JC (2017) The globalization of entrepreneurial litigation: law, culture, and incentives. Univ Pennsylvania Law Rev 165:1895–1925

Dumain SP (2005) Recent amendments to Rule 23. In: Practising Law Institute, Current developments in federal civil practice 2005. Litigation and Administrative Practice Course Handbook Series. Practising Law Institute Litigation, pp. 221–248

Edward CH (2002) Federal class action reform in the United States: past and future and where next? Defense Counsel J 69:432–440

Eisenberg T, Miller GP (2004) The role of opt-outs and objectors in class action litigation: theoretical and empirical issues. Vanderbilt Law Rev 57(5):1529–1570

Eizenga MA, Davis E (2011) A history of class actions: modern lessons from deep roots. Can Class Action Rev 7(1):3–31

Estagnan JS (2004) Las acciones colectivas de grupo. Aranzadi Civil-Mercantil 22/2003

Falla É (2014) The role of the court in collective redress litigation: comparative report. Larcier, Brussels

Fiedler L (2010) Class Actions zur Durchsetzung des europäischen Kartellrechts: Nutzen und mögliche prozessuale Ausgestaltung von kollektiven Rechtsschutzverfahren im deutschen Recht zur privaten Durchsetzung des europäischen Kartellrechts. Mohr Siebeck, Tübingen

Foer AA (2012) Cy pres as a remedy in private antitrust litigation. In: Foer AA Stutz RM (eds) Private enforcement of antitrust law in the United States. Edward Elgar, Cheltenham, pp 349–364

Geiger C (2015) Kollektiver Rechtsschutz im Zivilprozess: Die Gruppenklage zur Durchsetzung von Massenschäden und ihre Auswirkungen. Mohr Siebeck, Tübingen

Gidi A (2003) Class actions in Brazil—a model for civil law countries. Am J Compar Law 51(2):311–408

Gidi A (2012) The recognition of US class action judgments abroad: the case of Latin America. Brooklyn J Int Law 37(3):893–965

Greiner C (1998) Die Class Action im amerikanischen Recht und deutscher ordre public. Peter Lang, Frankfurt am Main

Gryphon M (2011) Assessing the effects of a "loser pays" rule on the American legal system: an economic analysis and proposal for reform. Rutgers J Law Public Policy 8(3):567–613

Halfmeier A (2012) Recognition of a WCAM settlement in Germany. Nederlands Int Privaatrecht (NIPR) 30(2):176–184

Hensler DR (2017) From sea to shining sea: how and why class actions are spreading globally. Univ Kansas Law Rev 65:965–988

Hodges Ch (2008) The reform of class and representative actions in European legal systems. Hart Publishing, Oxford

Issacharoff S, Miller GP (2009) Will aggregate litigation come to Europe? Vanderbilt Law Rev 62(1):179–210

Issacharoff S, Miller GP (2012) Will aggregate litigation come to Europe? In: Backhaus G, Cassone A, Ramello GB (eds) The law and economics of class actions in Europe: lessons from America. Edward Elgar, Cheltenham, pp 37–68

Jiménez JML (2008) Las acciones colectivas como medio de protección de los derechos e intereses de los consumidores. Diario La Ley, 6852, January 2008

Kalven H, Rosenfield M (1941) The contemporary function of the class suit. Univ Chicago Law Rev 8(4):684–721

Karlsgodt PG (2012) Chapter 1: United States. In: Karlsgodt PG (ed) World class actions: a guide to group and representative actions around the globe. Oxford University Press, Oxford, pp 3–55

Katzarsky A, Georgiev G (2012) Chapter 11: Bulgaria. In: Dodds-Smith I, Brown A (eds) The international comparative legal guide to class & group actions. Global Legal Group, London, pp 64–69

Kinsella K, Wheatman S (2010) Class notice and claims administration. In: Foer AA, Cuneo JW (eds) The international handbook on private enforcement of competition law. Edward Elgar, Cheltenham, pp 264–274

Kinsella K, Wheatman S (2012) Chapter 13—Class notice and claims administration. In: Foer AA, Stutz RM (eds) Private enforcement of antitrust law in the United States. Edward Elgar, Cheltenham, pp 338–348

Kiurunen P, Lindström N (2012) Chapter 9: Norway. In: Karlsgodt PG (ed) World class actions: a guide to group and representative actions around the globe. Oxford University Press, Oxford, pp 229–240

Koch H (2001) Non-class group litigation under EU and German law. Duke J Compar Int Law 11(2):355–367

Lange S (2011) Das begrenzte Gruppenverfahren: Konzeption eines Verfahrens zur Bewältigung von Großschäden auf der Basis des Kapitalanleger-Musterverfahrensgesetzes. Mohr Siebeck, Tübingen

López JJM (2001) Las acciones de clase en el Derecho español. InDret (3). http://www.indret.com/pdf/057_es.pdf. Accessed 20 April 2019

Magnier V, Alleweldt R (2008) Country report: France. In: Evaluation of the effectiveness and efficiency of collective redress mechanisms in the European Union. Civic Consulting & Oxford Economics

Mazen N-J (1987) Le recours collectif: réalité québécoise et projet français. Revue internationale de droit comparé 39(2):373–411

Mieres LJ (2000) Acerca de la constitucionalidad de la nueva regulación de las acciones colectivas promovidas por asociaciones de consumidores y usuarios. Barcelona

Mulheron R (2014) The class action in common law legal systems: a comparative perspective. Oxford University Press, Oxford

Nagy CI (2010) A csoportos igényérvényesítés összehasonlító jogi modelljei II. A csoportos igényérvényesítés európai modelljei és az összehasonlító jogi modellek tanulságai. Külgazdaság Jogi Melléklete 54(11):121–152

Nagy CI (2013) Comparative collective redress from a law and economics perspective: without risk there is no reward! Columbia J Eur Law 19(3):469–498

Nagy CI (2015) Le débat sur l'action collective en Europe: ils n'ont rien appris, ni rien oublié? Revue internationale de droit comparé 67(4):941–969

Pace NM (2008) Class actions in the United States of America: an overview of the process and the empirical literature. Globalclassaction. http://globalclassactions.stanford.edu/sites/default/files/documents/USA__National_Report.pdf. Accessed 20 April 2019

Piché C (2018) Class action value. Theor Inquiries Law 19:261–302

Piñeiro LC (2009) Las acciones colectivas y su eficacia extraterritorial. Universidade de Santiago de Compostela, Santiago de Compostela, Problemas de recepción y transplante de las class actions en Europa

Poisson E, Fléchet C (2012) 4.5.2. Proposed reforms in France in Chapter 4: representative actions and proposed reforms in the European Union. In: Karlsgodt P G (ed) World class actions: a guide to group and representative actions around the globe. Oxford University Press, Oxford

Rathod J, Vaheesan S (2016) The arc and architecture of private enforcement regimes in the United States and Europe: a view across the atlantic. Univ New Hampshire Law Rev 14:303–375

Rodger BJ (2011) Editorial—private enforcement and collective redress: the benefits of empirical research and comparative approaches. Competit Law Rev 8(1):1–6

Sherman EF (2002) Group litigation under foreign legal systems: variations and alternatives to American class action. DePaul Law Rev 52(2):401–432

Stadler A (2011) Mass Tort Litigation. In: Stürner R, Kawano M (eds) Comparative studies on business tort litigation. Mohr Siebeck, Tübingen, pp 163–175

Stadler A (2015) Die internationale Anerkennung von Urteilen und Vergleichen aus Verfahren des kollektiven Rechtsschutzes mit op-out Mechanismen. In: Geimer R, Kaissis A, Thümmel RC (eds) Ars Aequi et Boni in Mundo. Festschrift für Rolf A. Schütze zum 80. Geburtstag, pp. 561–578. CH Beck, München

Stephen FH, Love JH (2000) Regulation of the legal profession. In: Boudewijn B, de Geest G (eds) Encyclopedia of law and economics, vol 3. Elgar Publishing, Cheltenham

Strong SI (2013) Cross-border collective redress in the European Union: constitutional rights in the face of the Brussels I regulation. Arizona State Law Journal 45:233–279

Trebilcock MJ (1976) A study on consumer misleading and unfair trade practices, vol 1. Minister of Supply and Services, Ottawa

Trstenjak V (2015) Les mécanismes de recours collectif et leur importance pour la protection des consommateurs. In: Tizzano A, Rosas A, de Lapuerta RS, Lenaerts K, Kokott J (eds) La Cour de justice de l'Union européenne sous la présidence de Vassilios Skouris (2003–2015): liber amicorum Vassilios Skouris. Bruylant, Bruxelles, pp 681–696

Udvary S (2015) Pro actione collectiva – a komplex perlekedés amerikai eszközei, különösen a class action összehasonlító vizsgálata az intézmény magyarországi recepciója céljából. Patrocinium, Budapest

Waller SW (2015) The fall and rise of the antitrust class action. http://ssrn.com/abstract=2641867. Accessed 20 April 2019

Yeazell SC (1987) From medieval group litigation to the modern class action. Yale University Press, New Haven

Chapter 4
Transatlantic Perspectives: Comparative Law Framing

Not surprisingly, collective actions' regulatory contexts in the US and in Europe differ considerably. US law features a large array of legal institutions which catalyze the operation of class actions but are completely missing in Europe (e.g. contingency fees, no or one-way cost-shifting, super-compensatory damages such as punitive and treble damages, pre-trial discovery, jury trials). In fact, notwithstanding their independent nature, these legal concepts are quite often associated with class actions.[1]

The discovery of these contextual concepts is essential for two reasons. On the one hand, class actions are a real transplant and, as such, may have a quite different operation and impact in a new legal environment than in the US. On the other hand, class actions raise a good number of regulatory issues that simply do not emerge in the home country. For instance, due to the lack of cost-shifting, the allocation of liability for the prevailing defendant's legal costs is not an issue in US law, while it is a pivotal question in Europe.

This chapter, with the purpose of providing a comparative law framing, first, takes stock of the major differences between the regulatory and social environments of class actions on the two sides of the Atlantic. Second, it demonstrates how, as a consequence of these differences, class actions entail diverging outcomes in the US and Europe. Third, it presents the truly European issues raised by class actions, which are unknown for American law.

4.1 Disparate Regulatory Environments

One of the commonplaces of comparative law is that the transplantation of legal concepts is not like organ transplantation: legal institutions are deeply rooted in the legal system that gave life to them and are a coherent part of their legal, social and

---

[1] See Blennerhassett (2016: 132–133).

© The Author(s) 2019
C. I. Nagy, *Collective Actions in Europe*,
SpringerBriefs in Law, https://doi.org/10.1007/978-3-030-24222-0_4

cultural environment.[2] Hence, when assessing the potential consequences of introducing opt-out collective actions in Europe, the very first question to be addressed is the differences between the US class action and the European collective action in terms of context, in particular, because empirical data clearly suggests: the same opt-out collective action mechanism that bursts its banks in the US may only be a peaceful creek in Europe.

The ontological difference framing the comparative law analysis lies in the function of collective actions. In the US, private enforcement (individual and collective alike) may have both a compensatory and a public policy function. The concept of "private attorney general"[3] describes this expressively: the law privatizes a parcel of public enforcement and uses market forces to further public policy (while saving public resources). Albeit that class actions are an important element of this regulatory strategy, it embraces individual and collective actions alike. The key to this concept is the financial incentives offered by the law. For instance, in *Hawaii v. Standard Oil Co.*, the Supreme Court, referring to the treble damages available under US antitrust law, stressed that "[b]y offering potential litigants the prospect of a recovery in three times the amount of their damages, Congress encouraged these persons to serve as 'private attorneys general.'"[4]

On the contrary, the concept of "private attorney general" is completely alien to European law, where private enforcement is not meant to replace or supplement public enforcement and collective actions are confined merely to facilitating victims to acquire an effective private remedy. This implies that as long as this attitude is maintained, European collective actions cannot be expected to produce the same effectiveness in terms of enforcement as the US class action and their performance should be assessed in light of this consideration. The regulatory complexity of and resistance against collective actions may be traced back to the fact that Europe experiments with the importation of a mechanism that has a substantial public policy role to fulfill a purely compensatory function. Nonetheless, as demonstrated below, US class actions' public policy function is made up of a general set of contextual legal concepts and not the opt-out class action alone.

One of the most important dissimilarities is cultural and economic in essence and relates to the role of lawyers. The major difference between litigators on the two sides of the Atlantic is that "entrepreneurial lawyering" is virtually missing in Europe,[5] where the lawyer is a counsel, normally paid on an hourly or a flat-rate basis, and

---

[2]For an analysis on the culture of collective litigation, see Stier and Tzankova (2016).

[3]*Perma Life Mufflers, Inc. v. International Parts Corp.*, 392 U. S. 134, 147 (1968) (Fortas, J., concurring in result); Strong (2012: 900), Udvary (2013: 71).

[4]405 U.S. 251, 262 (1972).

[5]See Karlsgodt (2012: 49).

contingency fee arrangements are rare,[6] in some Member States even prohibited or restricted.[7] The lawyer usually does not take any risk in the action and law-suits are normally not financed (not even partially) by law firms. In contrast to this, US class actions are funded by lawyers and law firms, in exchange for a contingency fee.[8] US litigators enter contingency fee arrangements and, hence, take enormous risks.

In Europe, some jurisdictions prohibit only pure contingency fees, where the attorney's fee is linked exclusively to the outcome of the case and the attorney receives no remuneration in case of loss. For instance, French law expressly prohibits pure contingency fees, i.e. attorney's fees based exclusively on the outcome of the case, albeit a conditional reward, as a complimentary element, may be combined with a fixed fee.[9] Although the French Supreme Court (Cour de Cassation) held that a conditional reward does not need be proportionate to the fixed fee and may exceed the latter,[10] it is widely accepted that the fixed fee element may not be negligible. A similar approach is taken by Belgian[11] and Romanian law,[12] which prohibit agreements on fees that are exclusively linked to the outcome of the case but permit the stipulation of a complementary fee conditional on the outcome.

Some jurisdictions are more stringent and prohibit all agreements where the attorney's fee is somehow, even partially, linked to the outcome of the case. In Germany, contingency fees have been traditionally prohibited. The German Federal Constitutional Court (Bundesverfassungsgericht) held a decade ago that the categorical prohibition of contingency fee arrangements is unconstitutional but it was quick to add that this deficiency can be easily removed if creating an exception for cases where a fee (hourly fee or flat rate) would deter the plaintiff from pursuing his right by reason of his financial circumstances.[13] As a corollary, German law was amended to make it possible for the parties to agree to contingency fees but only in cases where the client, because of his economic circumstances, would otherwise not pursue his

---

[6]For a comparative overview, see e.g. Chieu (2010: 148), Russell (2010: 173).

[7]See Grace (2006: 287–88), Waelbroeck et al. (2004: 93–94, 116–17), Leskinen (2011: 98–105).

[8]See Hodges (2009: 42) ("[T]he claimant has no financial risk but has significant incentive to take action. In particular, any intermediary representing the claimant and funding the litigation has significant incentives."); Karlsgodt (2012: 53).

[9]Section 10 of Loi n° 71-1130 du 31 décembre 1971 portant réforme de certaines professions judiciaires et juridiques, version consolidée au 12 mars 2017.

[10]Cour de Cassation, Chambre civile 1, du 10 juillet 1995, 93-20.290.

[11]Section 446ter of the Judicial Code (Code judiciaire).

[12]Section 130 of Statutul profesiei de avocat, Adoptat prin Hotărârea Consiliului U.N.B.R. nr. 64/2011 privind adoptarea Statutului profesiei de avocat (M. Of. nr. 898 din 19 decembrie 2011). See ICCJ. Decizia nr. 2131/2013. Civil. Constatare nulitate act. Recurs.

[13]Beschluss des Ersten Senats vom 12. Dezember 2006. 1 BvR 2576/04.

claim.[14] Nonetheless, as a matter of practice, contingency fee arrangements are still rare in Germany.

Not surprisingly, the Code of Conduct for European Lawyers of the Council of Bars and Law Societies of Europe (CCBE),[15] in principal, pronounces contingency fee agreements (pactum de quota litis) unethical, unless it "is in accordance with an officially approved fee scale or under the control of competent authority having jurisdiction over the lawyer."[16]

Interestingly, in Spain, the ethical prohibition of contingency fee arrangements was quashed in 2008: the Spanish Supreme Court considered the Spanish Bar Association's ban on contingency fees as restrictive of competition and abolished them.[17] However, contingency fee arrangements are, as a matter of practice, rare.

Whatever the precise national rules and the specific limits are, most importantly, contingency fees are still not generally accepted in Europe and there is no market providing litigation services on this basis.

In the same vein, in most European countries, active client-acquiring and lawyer advertisements are banned or heavily restricted,[18] while, in the US, cases are often not client- but lawyer-driven[19] and this is all the more true in class actions.[20]

Furthermore, not only lawyers but also clients are different. The statistical data suggests that the American society is much more litigious than the European.[21]

In short, in the US, there is an industry that assumes the risks of litigation in exchange for an appropriate risk premium. On the other hand, in Europe there is no

---

[14]Rechtsanwaltsvergütungsgesetz vom 5. Mai 2004 (BGBl. I S. 718, 788), last amended through Section 13 of Gesetz vom 21. November 2016 (BGBl. I S. 2591), Gesetz über die Vergütung der Rechtsanwältinnen und Rechtsanwälte (Rechtsanwaltsvergütungsgesetz—RVG), § 4a Erfolgshonorar: "Quota litis (Section 49b(2), first sentence of the [German] Federal Lawyers' Act (Bundesrechtsanwaltsordnung—BRAO)) may be agreed only for an individual case and only if the client, upon reasonable consideration, would be deterred from taking legal proceedings without the agreement of quota litis on account of his economic situation. In court proceedings, it may be agreed that in case of failure, no remuneration, or a lower amount than the statutory remuneration, is to be paid if it is agreed that an appropriate supplement is to be paid on the statutory remuneration in case of success." Bundesrechtsanwaltsordnung in der im Bundesgesetzblatt Teil III, Gliederungsnummer 303-8, veröffentlichten bereinigten Fassung, last amended through Section 3 of Gesetz vom 19. Februar 2016 (BGBl. I S. 254), § 49b(2).

[15]https://www.ccbe.eu/NTCdocument/EN_CCBE_CoCpdf1_1382973057.pdf. Accessed 20 April 2019.

[16]Section 3.3. Interestingly, in 2008, the Spanish Supreme Court found the Spanish Bar Association's ban on contingency fees restrictive of competition and quashed it.

[17]Sentencia del Tribunal Supremo, Sala de lo Contencioso-Administrativo, de 4 noviembre 2008 JUR\2009\2800, Recurso de Casación 5837/2005.

[18]While lawyer advertising is interdicted or restricted in several EU Member States, in the last period these have been eliminated in several legal systems. See Communication from the Commission: Report on Competition in Professional Services, COM (2004) 83 final, 14; Stephen and Love (2000: 987–1017).

[19]See Calabresi and Schwartz (2011: 178–79) ("The business cases are almost entirely lawyer-driven.").

[20]See Alexander (2000: 12).

[21]See Gryphon (2011: 1).

established industry to assume the litigation risks, partially because European legal systems skimp litigators in financial rewards and incentives.

The shifting of legal costs is a pivotal question of class actions.[22] According to the "American rule", each party bears his own costs and attorney's fees cannot be shifted.[23] The plaintiff does not run the risk of paying the defendant's attorney if losing the action; and likewise, the defendant does not have to reimburse the winning plaintiff for his legal costs. It is true that US law contains plentiful exceptions providing for the shifting of reasonable attorney's fees, but these rules mainly enable one-way costs shifting from the prevailing plaintiff to the losing defendant.[24] Though the prevailing defendant may request the court to shift the attorney's fees onto the unsuccessful plaintiff, this is limited to exceptional cases, such as frivolous law-suits where the plaintiff acted in bad faith.[25] In other words, in the US, as a matter of practice, the plaintiff does not run the risk of becoming liable for the prevailing defendant's attorney's fees.

In contrast to this, as most parts of the world, European jurisdictions traditionally follow the principle of two-way cost-shifting,[26] albeit shiftable legal costs are often limited and rarely cover all the expenses. In Europe, "the winner takes it all" and the loser, at least theoretically, pays all the legal costs that were induced by the proceedings, irrespective of whether these emerged on the plaintiff's or on the defendant's side.[27]

Of course, cost-shifting is never perfect and never all-embracing; but this is the principle. Some jurisdictions content themselves with limiting the shiftable sum to reasonable legal costs. In Hungarian law, the principle is full reimbursement and it is at the court's discretion whether and to what extent it shifts the prevailing party's attorney's fees. The losing party is liable for all the necessary legal costs that have a causal link to the claim's judicial enforcement, irrespective of whether they emerged

---

[22]Waelbroeck et al. (2004: 92–95). For a law and economics analysis of the American rule and the European two-way cost shifting principle, see Carbonara and Parisi (2012).

[23]See Rule 54(d) of the Federal Rules of Civil Procedure. *Alyeska Pipeline Service Co. v. Wilderness Society*, 421 US 240 (1975).

[24]See e.g. Sherman Act, 15 USC. § 4304(a); Fair Labor Standards Act, 29 USC. § 216; Magnuson–Moss Warranty Act, 15 USC. § 2310(d)(2).

[25]See Rule 11 of the Federal Rules of Civil Procedure; *Roadway Express, Inc. v. Piper*, 447 US 752, (1980); *Hall v. Cole*, 412 US 1, 5 (1973); Sherman Act, 15 USC. § 4304(a)(2).

[26]An exception that confirms the rule may be found in the Bulgarian administrative competition procedure. Section 69(2) of the Bulgarian Act on protection of competition provides for one-way cost-shifting. "Where the Commission [on Protection of Competition] issues a decision establishing an infringement under this Law, the Commission shall order the infringer to pay the costs of the proceedings, if so requested by the other party. If no infringement is established, the costs shall be borne by the parties who incurred them." The Act was promulgated in the State Gazette's Issue 102 of 28 November 2008. For an English translation see http://www.wipo.int/wipolex/en/text.jsp?file_id=238274. Accessed on 20 April 2019.

[27]Waelbroeck et al. (2004: 92–95). For a law and economics analysis of the American and the English (or continental) rule, see Carbonara and Parisi (2012).

before or during the law-suit.[28] The prevailing party may claim reimbursement for the attorney's fees stipulated in the mandate agreement. However, the court may reduce the shiftable attorney's fees, if it is not proportionate to the claim's value or the actual work done.[29] Likewise, in Bulgaria, the losing party my seek reduction of the attorney's fees claimed by the prevailing party, if it is exorbitant taking into account the value and complexity of the case.[30] German law also provides for the shifting of reasonable legal costs on the losing party,[31] however, the recoverable attorney's fees is capped by a statutory schedule.[32] In French law, attorney's fees, which normally make up the overwhelming majority of the expenses, are shifted on the losing party to the extent determined by the court, which has to allocate them in an equitable manner and taking into account the losing party's financial situation.[33]

The "American rule" combined with the wide-spread use of contingency fee arrangements and the entrepreneurial law firm model creates a very peculiar compound that lies at the heart of the American litigation system. The plaintiff is very motivated to litigate: he faces no risk; all hazards are devolved upon his lawyer (contingency fee) and the defendant ("American rule").[34] On the other hand, in Europe, the plaintiff, normally, cannot transfer the risks related to his own legal representation onto his lawyer, who works on the basis of an hourly rate, and has to compensate the defendant for his legal costs, if the court decides against the plaintiff.

Finally, US awards are much more generous for plaintiffs who sustained damages due to pernicious or malicious practices. Punitive[35] and treble damages and "pain and suffering" awards are magnets that are non-existent in Europe. The availability of super-compensatory remedies and intensely generous "pain and suffering" awards may make litigation more attractive in cases where the balance of the litigation's expected value and expected costs is negative.

---

[28] Sections 80 and 83(1) of Act CXXX of 2016 on the Civil Procedure (2016. évi CXXX. törvény a polgári perrendtartásról).

[29] Section 2 of Ministry of Justice Decree nr 32 of 22 August 2003 on the attorney's costs that may be established in judicial proceedings (32/2003. (VIII. 22.) IM rendelet a bírósági eljárásban megállapítható ügyvédi költségekről).

[30] Section 78(5) Bulgarian Code of Civil Procedure, for an English version of the statutory text, see https://kenarova.com/law/Code%20of%20Civil%20Procedure.pdf. Accessed 20 April 2019.

[31] Section 91 of the German Code of Civil Procedure (Zivilprozessordnung), Zivilprozessordnung in der Fassung der Bekanntmachung vom 5. Dezember 2005 (BGBl. I S. 3202; 2006 I S. 431; 2007 I S. 1781), last amended through Section of the Gesetz vom 21. November 2016 (BGBl. I S. 2591).

[32] Rechtsanwaltsvergütungsgesetz vom 5. Mai 2004 (BGBl. I S. 718, 788), last amended through Section 13 of Gesetz vom 21. November 2016 (BGBl. I S. 2591).

[33] Sections 695-700 of the French Code of Civil Procedure (Code de la procédure civile). For a detailed analysis, see Gjidara-Decaix (2010: 325).

[34] See Hodges (2009: 42).

[35] Black's Law Dictionary 416-19 (8th ed. 2004) ("damages" and "punitive damages"); *BMW of N. Am., Inc. v. Gore*, 517 US 559 (1996); *Cooper Indus. v. Leatherman Tool Grp., Inc.*, 532 US 424, 432 (2001). On the interaction and combination of punitive damages and class actions from a law and economics perspective, see Parisi and Cenini (2008).

In the US, punitive damages are generally available in all but five states[36] and treble damages are provided for in various state and federal statutes. While surveys suggest that punitive damages are awarded infrequently[37] and "are not typically very large",[38] they are an integral part of the US justice system. The purpose of punitive damages is *"to punish* (…) [the wrongdoer] for his outrageous conduct and *to deter* him and others like him from similar conduct in the future."[39] The amount of damages orientates to the gravity of the mischief ("the defendant's act, the nature and extent of the harm to the plaintiff that the defendant caused or intended to cause and the wealth of the defendant")[40] and not to the weight of the harm.

On the other hand, in continental Europe, these goals and this rationale are, in principle, reserved for criminal law and damages are meant (only) to compensate the injured party for the loss suffered and may under no circumstance entail his enrichment: the purpose of damages is to restore the initial status (in integrum restitutio), that is, to compensate; they are not destined to punish the wrongdoer, although they may certainly have such a side-effect.[41] The Principles of European Tort Law, which are both a restatement of the common core of European tort law and also a proposal for a comprehensive system of tortious liability, stress the compensatory purpose of damages and treat their deterrent effects as a welcome by-product.

> Damages are a money payment to compensate the victim, that is to say, to restore him, so far as money can, to the position he would have been in if the wrong complained of had not been committed. Damages also serve the aim of preventing harm.[42]

Interestingly, while exemplary damages are, theoretically, available under English common law, in *Rookes v Barnard*,[43] the English Supreme Court (at that time: House of Lords) almost fully evirated the legal doctrine that underlay the remarkable conceptual development in the US resulting in the current practice of punitive awards. It held that exemplary damages, aside from the case when they are provided for by a statute, can be awarded only in matters involving "oppressive, arbitrary or unconstitutional action by the servants of the government" and when "the Defendant's conduct has been calculated by him to make a profit for himself which may well exceed the compensation payable to the plaintiff."[44]

---

[36] Sebok (2009: 155). See Rustada (2005: 1297).

[37] Surveys suggest that punitive damages were awarded in 2–9% of all cases where plaintiffs won. Sebok (2007: 964–965).

[38] Sebok (2009: 156–158).

[39] Restatement of Torts, Second, §908 (emphasis added).

[40] Id.

[41] See e.g. BGH 4 June 1992, BGHZ 118, 312 (Bundesgerichtshof). Quotations refer to the translation in Wegen and Sherer (1993) 1320 ("[O]ften, the sole appropriate aim of the civil action taken in response to an illegal act is to compensate for the effects of that act on the financial circumstances of the parties directly concerned"); Isidro (2009) 246.

[42] Principles of European Tort Law. Text and Commentary. European Group on Tort Law. 2009, Article 10:101 (Nature and purpose of damages).

[43] *Rookes v Barnard* [1964] 1 All England Law Reports (All ER) 367.

[44] On exemplary damages in English law, see Wilcox (2009: 7–53).

Finally, it is worth briefly highlighting that the differences between the American and European patterns of civil procedure also have a significant but less quantifiable effect on the operation of collective litigation: plaintiff-friendly US discovery rules significantly contribute to the success of class actions, while the lack of them may choke off collective actions in Europe. Jury trials, a scheme almost never used in Europe, certainly add to the uncertainty of outcomes but probably to the detriment of the defendants.

The above mapping of the contextual differences points out that in a civil-law environment collective actions obviously do not work in the same way as they do in the US. This also implies that when evaluating opt-out collective actions from a European perspective, one has to distinguish its effects and operation from those of the contextual legal doctrines of US law. These are not specific to class actions and govern individual litigation too.[45] Furthermore, because of the different regulatory environment, in Europe, collective actions raise various novel questions that simply do not emerge in the US.

4.2   Why Should Europeans Not Fear the American Cowboy? Diverging Effects of Disparate Regulatory Environments

The major criticism against the US class action is that, through aggregation of individual claims, it creates a big, centrally conducted giant claim that makes the defendants settle even if the claim is unfounded (blackmailing potential).[46] "Blackmail settlements" are "settlements induced by a small probability of an immense judgment in a class action."[47] Nonetheless, both theoretical and empirical arguments suggest that this aspect of US class actions would not emerge in a European environment.[48]

---

[45] Neumann and Magnusson (2011: 157), Nagy (2013: 482–485).

[46] See Ebbing (2004: 39), Weinstein (1997: 834), Calabresi and Schwartz (2011: 175), Posner (1973: 399, 2001: 925), Delatre (2011: 53). See also *In re Rhone-Poulenc Rorer, Inc.*, 51 F.3d 1293, 1299–1300 (7th Cir. 1995), *cert. denied* 116 S. Ct. 184 (1995); *West v. Prudential Secs., Inc.*, 282 F.3d 935, 937 (7th Cir. 2002).

[47] *In re Rhone-Poulenc*, 51 F.3d 1293, 1298 (1995), citing Friendly (1973: 120).

[48] See Hodges (2010: 374) ("The crucial fact that legislators and commentators failed to observe was that the American legal and constitutional system operates on a model that is fundamentally different from the European systems, in that it places considerable reliance on private enforcement as a substitute for public enforcement. The result is that the American and European systems are incomparable in many respects."). Smithka (2009: 189–190). Unfortunately, it is usually taken as granted, without any empirical evidence, that opt-out collective proceedings, by themselves, generate excesses. See Delatre (2011: 38), Buchner (2015: 51–57). For the demythologization of the claim that third-party financing of class actions entails frivolous litigation in the US, see Hensler (2014).

It has to be noted that the effectiveness and widespread use of collective litigation and the potential for abuse and adverse effects are inversely proportional to each other: the engine of US class actions is the risk premium the group representative is afforded, while the risk premium may increase the potential for abuse and adverse effects. This issue will be addressed in Sect. 4.3.

It is submitted that the efficient cause of the perceived blackmailing potential of US class actions is that, among others, due to the "American rule" and the availability of super-compensatory damages, there is a striking imbalance (to the defendant's detriment) between the litigation's expected value and expected costs and, hence, it is rational for the defendant to settle even if the claim is grossly unfounded. Namely, due to the "American rule" (i.e. each party bears his own legal costs), the law-suit unavoidably causes serious losses to the defendant, irrespective of whether he wins the case or not. This is topped by the availability of super-compensatory damages.

The diverging effects of the above disparate regulatory environments may be best shown through a numerical demonstration. It has to be stressed that these calculations are valid as to both individual and collective claims. The only difference between collective litigation and individual actions is that the former amalgamates different claims. That is, the diverging effects of the disparate regulatory environments work irrespective of whether it is an individual or a collective action. This confirms that the alleged excesses of class actions are not due to the opt-out rule itself but to its regulatory environment.[49] Hence, it seems to be unconvincing that the above phenomenon is problematic in case of collective actions but not in case of individual litigation.

The calculation in Sect. 3.1.4. demonstrates well how the legal institutions surrounding US class actions tilt the balance in the plaintiff's favor (independent of whether it is an individual or a collective plaintiff). Recall that in the antitrust case used for the purpose of the foregoing demonstration the plaintiff had a claim in value of $1,000,000, while legal costs were $200,000 − 200,000 for the plaintiff and the defendant; the plaintiff's chance to prevail was 10%. Because it was an antitrust case coming under the Sherman Act, treble damages were available[50] and the plaintiff benefitted from one-way cost shifting (reimbursement for reasonable attorney's fees).

In such an extremely weak case, it is reasonable for the plaintiff to sue and for the defendant to settle; what is more, although the plaintiff has only 10% chance to win, the defendant may reasonably accept a settlement of more than 50% of the claim's value.

A reasonable plaintiff's decision on whether or not to sue would rest on the following calculation. The plaintiff's costs are $200,000. The expected value of the law-suit is made up of two components. First, the principal claim which amounts to $1,000,000 and has to be tripled due to the treble damages rule ($3,000,000).

---

[49]Nagy (2013: 482–495).

[50]Though statutory provisions prescribing treble damages are relatively rare and punitive damages claims are more common, treble damages are used for the purpose of calculation, as in case of punitive damages outcomes are less predictable.

Second, the plaintiff may expect reimbursement for his reasonable attorney's fees which amount to $200,000. That is, if he wins, the plaintiff gets $3,200,000, however, both items of income may occur with a probability of 10%. Accordingly, the expected value is $320,000 = ($1.000.000 × 3 + $200.000) × 10%, and the balance between the plaintiff's costs and the expected value is $ +120,000 = $320,000 − $200,000. In other words, the balance is positive, it is reasonable for the plaintiff to sue and to accept a settlement offer higher than $ 120,000.

The defendant's side is the inverse of the above calculus, but, contrary to the plaintiff's situation, the balance of litigation is always negative: the defendant has to inevitably bear the legal costs, these cannot be shifted on the plaintiff even if the latter loses the case, while the defendant cannot expect any income in the event he wins. Furthermore, the defendant also runs the risk of losing the case, even if the probability of this is rather small.

As a corollary, the defendant has no expected value: the defendant may expect no reimbursement for his reasonable attorney's fees. The expected costs are made up of the following two items. First, the defendant will incur legal expenses in value of $ 200,000. Second, there is a 10% probability that the defendant has to pay treble damages to the plaintiff in value of $ 3,000,000 and reimbursement for the plaintiff's reasonable attorney's fees in value of $ 200,000. Altogether, the defendant's balance is $ −520,000 = $ −200.000 + ($ −1,000,000 × 3 + $ −200,000) × 10%. In other words, the balance is negative, it is reasonable for the defendant to settle and to accept a settlement offer lower than $520,000, although the plaintiff has only 10% chance to prevail as to a $ 1,000,000 claim.

If the parties act reasonably, they should settle the case between $120,000 and $520,000. The settlement value will depend on their bargaining skills and tactics.

Let us see how the above case would work in a European legal environment. Here, it would not be reasonable for the plaintiff to sue. The plaintiff's expected value is 10% of the principal claim: $100,000 = $1,000,000 × 10%. His expected costs are made up of the legal costs of both parties: if he loses, he will be liable for all the legal costs: $400,000 = 2 × $200,000; if he wins, at least theoretically, he will incur no legal costs as the expenses advanced by him will be reimbursed by the losing defendant. Taking into account that he has 90% chance to lose, the expected costs are $360,000 = $400,000 × 90%. Accordingly, the plaintiff's balance is $−260,000 = $100,000 − $360,000. In other words, the balance is negative and, hence, it is not reasonable for the plaintiff to sue.

The above calculations demonstrate well that, as noted above, the perceived excesses of class actions (e.g. black-mailing potential, forced settlements, litigation in extremely weak cases) are, in fact, not due to the opt-out class action itself but to the surrounding US regulatory environment, represented by doctrines like treble damages, the American rule and one-way cost shifting. Accordingly, these diverging effects emerge irrespective of whether it is an individual or a collective action and are not concomitant with the opt-out class action itself.

Interestingly, and perversely, the American rule makes the defendant's balance in a case with a probability of plaintiff success lower than 50% comparatively worse and the defendant comparatively more inclined to settle than in a case with a probability of plaintiff success over 50%. Below a 50% likelihood of plaintiff success, in the US the defendant will have a greater incentive to settle than in Europe, while over this threshold, a US defendant is comparatively less likely to settle than the European defendant. The reason behind this is the non-shiftability of legal costs. Assume, for the sake of simplicity, that the two sides have legal costs of the same value. The "American rule" makes the defendant bear 50% of the overall legal costs even in cases where the plaintiff's probability of success is less than 50% and, hence, in Europe, the expected legal costs would be below 50%. Likewise, the "American rule" makes the defendant bear 50% of the proceedings' overall legal costs (but not more) also in cases where the plaintiff's probability of success is more than 50% and, hence, in Europe, the expected legal costs to be borne by the defendant would be over 50%. Accordingly, the "American rule" incites defendants to settle against less substantiated claims more than the "loser pays" rule, while it incites them comparatively less in the event the plaintiff has a very good case.

Fortunately, the above theoretical analysis is not left without an empirical crutch. There are numerous opt-out systems in Europe: perhaps surprisingly, representation without a power of attorney is neither beyond example, nor exceptional.[51] As shown below, the available statistical data reinforce the above analysis and show that in Europe opt-out systems do not produce the effects they trigger in the US. Furthermore, Australia and Canada introduced US-style class actions, while their legal systems diverge in several relevant aspects from the US regulatory environment and are in line with the principles prevailing in Europe. Accordingly, the empirical experiments of these countries may provide some guidance.

---

[51] See Delatre (2011: 38) ("[I]t is impossible to readily exclude a model of collective redress on the ground that it would not be consistent with the European experience on the topic. Essentially every model of collective litigation may be found in Europe, and the somewhat controversial opt-out class action does not constitute an exception.").

Opt-out group proceedings are available in Belgium,[52] Bulgaria,[53] Denmark,[54] France,[55] Greece,[56] Hungary,[57] Portugal,[58] Slovenia,[59]

---

[52]The Belgian system leaves it to the judge to decide whether the action should be carried out in the opt-in or the opt-out scheme. Law Inserting Title 2 on "Collective Compensation Action" in Book XVII "Special Jurisdictional Procedures" of the Code of Economic Law, 28 March 2014, Moniteur Belge (M.B.) (Official Gazette of Belgium (29 March 2014) (Loi portant insertion d'un titre 2 «De l'action en réparation collective» au livre XVII «Procédures juridictionnelles particulières» du Code de droit économique et portant insertion des définitions propres au livre XVII dans le livre 1er du Code de droit économique) and Section XVII.38 in conjunction with Section I.21 of the Belgian Code of Economic Law.

[53]Chapter 33, Sections 379-388 of the Bulgarian Code of Civil Procedure, for an English version of the statutory text, see https://kenarova.com/law/Code%20of%20Civil%20Procedure.pdf. Accessed 20 April 2019. See Katzarsky and Georgiev (2012: 64).

[54]Sections 254a-254e of the Administration of Justice Act.

[55]In France, de facto opt-out class actions were first introduced in the field of consumer protection in 2014, Loi n° 2014-344 du 17 mars 2014 relative à la consommation et Décr. n° 2014-1081 du 24 sept. 2014 relatif à l'action de groupe en matière de consommation, followed by the health care sector in January 2016, Loi n° 2016-41 du 26 janv. 2016 de modernisation de notre système de santé et Décr. n° 2016-1249 du 26 sept. 2016 relatif à l'action de groupe en matière de santé. In November 2016, a general framework was created in France for group actions. Loi n° 2016-1547 du 18 novembre 2016 de modernisation de la justice du XXIe siècle, JORF n°0269 du 19 novembre 2016 texte n° 1. The new regime extended the purview of the mechanism to discrimination, environmental and personal data and health care matters, inserting Sections 826-2-826-24 into the French Code of Civil Procedure.

[56]Articles 10(16)-(29) of Law 2251/1994 on Consumers' Protection. For an English translation, see https://www.eccgreece.gr/wp-content/uploads/2015/07/N2251-1994-enc2007-en1.pdf.

[57]Section 92 of Hungarian Competition Act (1996. évi LVII. törvény a tisztességtelen piaci magatartás és a versenykorlátozás tilalmáról); Sections 38-38/A of Hungarian Consumer Protection Act (Act CLV of 1997) (1997. évi CLV. törvény a fogyasztóvédelemről); Sections 580-591 of the new Hungarian Code of Civil Procedure effective as from 1 January 2018 (Act CXXX of 2016 on the Code of Civil Procedure, in Hungarian: 2016. évi CXXX. törvény a polgári perrendtartásról).

[58]Law 83/95 on the Acção Popular. See Rossi and Ferro (2013: 46–64), Ferro (2015: 299–300).

[59]Law on Collective Actions (Zakon o kolektivnih tožbah—ZkolT), Official Journal of the Republic of Slovenia No. 55/2017. For the English version of the statutory text, see http://www.pisrs.si/Pis.web/pregledPredpisa?id=ZAKO7399. Accessed 20 April 2019.

Spain,[60] and the United Kingdom[61] without having produced any litigation boom. Section 5.1 gives an account of the statistics of European class actions in these Member States and demonstrates that these systems brought about no litigation boom and, due to the lack of appropriate financial incentives, are not particulary effective or wide-spread and do not even compare to the US class action in terms of significance.

Since European empirical experiences are rather limited in terms of territorial representation and time, it is worth taking a look at systems outside the EU that adopted the US-style class action but have a regulatory environment that is in some relevant aspects different from the US. Australia and several provinces of Canada adopted US-style class action legislation and inserted it into a regulatory context where entrepreneurial law-firms, contingency fee arrangements and jury trials, though definitely existent, are less relevant, the allocation of legal costs is, as a general principle, governed by the "loser pays" rule, and the availability of super-compensatory damages is, in comparison to the US, highly restricted.[62] Presumably due to this regulatory environment, here the opt-out class action did not entail the overgrowth and abuses some perceive in the US.[63]

In Australia, opt-out class actions were introduced on the federal level in 1991 (these provisions entered into force on 4 March 1992)[64] and in the state of Victoria in 2000.[65] A 2009 study showed that 241 class action applications were filed up to March 2009 and 245 up to 30 June 2009; that is, on average, 14 class actions were instituted annually. The number of class action proceedings was fluctuant and their frequency did not have an increasing tendency. The first quarter of the rules' 17-year-long history saw 33 proceedings, followed by an intensive period of 92 proceedings;

---

[60]See Section 20 of Law 26/1984 of 19 July on Consumer Protection (Ley para la defensa de los consumidores y usuarios), now Section 24 of Royal Legislative Decree 1/2007 of 16 November, which issued a consolidated text of the Law on Consumer Protection and other supplementary laws (Texto refundido de la Ley General para la Defensa de los Consumidores y Usuarios y otras leyes complementarias). This provision was later on inserted in almost every special consumer law issued by the Spanish legislator. See Piñeiro (2007: 63–65). The Spanish Civil Procedure Act of 2000 is, though, the first attempt to systematize collective proceedings and its provisions (Articles 6, 11, 15, 15bis, 221, 222(2), 256(1)(6), 519).

[61]See e.g. Sections 18-19 of the 2002 Enterprise Act, which were inserted in Sections 47/A-47/D of the 1998 Competition Act. See also Group Litigation Orders in Sections 19.10. and 19.11. of the Civil Procedure Rules.

[62]See Heffernan (2003: 104), Branch and Montrichard (2005). See Gotanda (2004).

[63]See Stuyck et al. (2007: 379) ("Connected with concerns about (…) unmeritorious claims are fears that introducing US-type collective actions into a legal system would have a floodgate effect. That is, courts would be overwhelmed with weak cases trying to obtain compensation through collective action procedures. Experience from countries such as Sweden, Canada and Australia shows that the fears of legal blackmail and a resulting floodgate effect on the courts do not seem to have occurred."). Another point of reference could be Latin-America; several Latin-American countries adopted class action legislation and inserted this institution into a civil-law environment. See Gidi (2003: 311, 2012: 901–940).

[64]Federal Court of Australia Amendment Act 1991 (Cth). The federal class action rules are to be found in the Federal Court of Australia Act 1976 (Cth) pt IVA. See Clark and Harris (2001: 289).

[65]Supreme Court Act 1986 (Vic) pt 4A (Austl.). See Morabito (2009a: 321).

the number of the proceedings was decreasing in the last two quarters: 63 between 4 September 2000 and 3 December 2004 and 53 between 4 December 2004 and 3 March 2009.[66]

In Canada, opt-out class actions were introduced in the vast majority of the provinces (starting with Quebec's 1978 legislation[67])[68] and in the Federal Court Rules (in 2002).[69] Albeit class action litigation is frequent in Canada, it is by no means excessive, as compared to the US. Nonetheless, it is worthy of remark that Canada's empirical experiences may be taken into account only with some correction. For instance, contingency fees are lawful in Canada and lawyers fund the bulk of class actions[70]; and several provinces lifted or softened the "loser pays" principle in respect to class actions.[71]

Between 2010 and 2018, the launch of 826 class actions was reported to the Canadian Bar Association's database.[72] This is, on average, 92 cases *per annum*.[73] Other surveys show that at least 287 class action proposals were filed in Ontario between 1993 and April 2001[74] and, up to September 2004, 52 proposed class actions were certified in British Columbia, 104 in Ontario and 130 in Québec.[75] In another

---

[66] Morabito (2009b).

[67] Loi sur le recours collectif, L.Q. 1978, c. 8. See Bouchard (1980), Mazen (1987), Lafond (1998–1999: 19–34).

[68] British Columbia, Class Proceedings Act, R.S.B.C. 1996, c. 50; Newfoundland, Class Actions Act, S.N.L. 2001 c. C-18.1; Saskatchewan, Class Actions Act, R.S.S. 2001 c. C-12.01; Alberta, Class Proceedings Act, R.S.A. 2003 c. C-16.5; Manitoba, Class Proceedings Act, R.S.M. 2002 c. C130; New Brunswick, Class Proceedings Act, R.S.N.B. 2011 c. C-125; Nova Scotia, Class Proceedings Act, R.S.N.S. 2007 c. 28.

[69] Kalajdzic et al. (2009: note 29). For an overview of the Canadian experiences and major issues, see Watson (2001: 272–284).

[70] Kalajdzic et al. (2009: 44).

[71] Kalajdzic et al. (2009: 42). British Columbia essentially adopted the "American rule:" cost awards may be made only in case of "vexatious, frivolous or abusive conduct," improper or unnecessary applications or steps "taken for the purpose of delay or increasing costs or for any other improper purpose" and in case there are "exceptional circumstances that make it unjust to deprive the successful party of costs." See Class Proceedings Act, R.S.B.C. 1995 c. 50, art. 37 and Watson (2001: 274). In Ontario, the court, when exercising its discretion with respect to awarding costs, "may consider whether the class proceeding was a test case, raised a novel point of law or involved a matter of public interest." Class Proceedings Act, R.S.O. 1992, c. 6, s. 31(1).

[72] National Class Action Database, The Canadian Bar Association, http://www.cba.org/ ClassActions/main/gate/index/default.aspx. Accessed 20 April 2019. The database is based on voluntary reporting and is therefore not a comprehensive record of all Canadian class action lawsuits. Nonetheless, it may be used as a rough indicator as to the number of class actions in Canada within specific time periods.

[73] 2010: 116, 2011: 101, 2012: 141, 2013: n/a, 2014: 150, 2015: 85, 2016: 71, 2017: 80, 2018: 82.

[74] Baert and Guindon (2008: 3).

[75] For further statistics, see Branch and Montrichard (2005) and Lafond (2006: 35) (In Québec, between 1979 and 2004, 151 class actions ended with a settlement, and in 32 cases the court decided for the class).

survey, approximately 332 class actions were reported pending in 2009 and 427 class actions in 2014.[76]

Although these numbers do not exclude the potential of blackmail settlements and other adverse effects, they clearly suggest that collective proceedings entailed no litigation boom and the concern of blackmailing litigation seems not to be real.

4.3 The Novel Questions of Collective Actions in Europe

Collective actions are legal transplants alien to traditional civil-law thinking, hence, once introduced, they call for the re-consideration of a wide array of questions.[77] Obviously, it is perfectly legitimate to adopt foreign legal solutions without adopting their regulatory context; however, in this case, the legal transplant may raise issues that do not emerge in the donor country.

4.3.1 Funding in the Absence of One-Way Cost-Shifting, Contingency Fees and Punitive Damages

European legal systems are largely devoid of the financial incentives that so intensively stimulate litigation in the US (contingency fees, super-compensatory damages, no or one-way costs shifting). While it is neither imperative, nor necessarily justified to adopt foreign legal solutions as a package, absent this a foreign transplant may take a life of its own. In the US, class actions are normally financed by law firms (incited by the reward of a contingency fee) and protected against the risks related to the defendant's attorney's fees (due to the American rule). On the other hand, in Europe there is no comparable market, not only because class actions have no history but also because litigation is less profitable. In the US, law firms are compensated, via legal institutions of general application, for the immense risks they undertake. At the same time, there are no such mechanisms on the other side of the Atlantic. This circumstance calls for a regulatory consideration, given that financing is the oil in the engine of collective actions.[78]

Unfortunately, European collective action laws have failed to settle or even address the problem of financing. On the one had, they ruled out the American institutions that stimulated the operation of US class actions. On the other hand, they failed to replace these with appropriate substitutes. Nonetheless, European collective actions will not be effective and self-sustaining absent appropriate financial incentives providing a risk premium that compensates the group representative for the risks incurred.

---

[76]Kalajdzic (2018: 16–17).
[77]On the financing options in Europe, see Voet (2016: 201–222).
[78]See Nagy (2015: 548–550).

The European fear of the American-style financial incentives has been so huge that the Recommendation on Collective Redress suggested the introduction of safeguards in order to obviate incentives to abuse the mechanism of collective action. It makes the use of the "loser pays" principle mandatory,[79] excludes, at least in principle, contingency fees[80] and prohibits punitive damages.[81] Furthermore, it restricts group representation to non-profit entities.[82]

The Recommendation demonstrates well Europe's aversion to the American litigation pattern. Namely, these safeguards appear to be excessive (even redundant), taking into account that the Recommendation explains the choice of the "opt-in" system with the consideration of obviating abusive practices. The Recommendation's insistence on not adopting legal concepts peculiar to the US regulatory environment surrounding the operation of the US class action actually suggests that, on the other side of the Atlantic, it is not the opt-out system but its legal environment that may be responsible for the alleged plethora of class actions. Furthermore, contingency fees and punitive (or exemplary) damages are available in quite of few Member States[83] and there is no reason to rule them out specifically in relation to class actions. Albeit that the amount of exemplary damages awarded in European common law systems is tiny (as compared to US punitive awards), this concept is a solid part of these.[84]

The biggest trouble is, however, that the European model, in essence, rules out the risk premium devices of US law, which are rather unpopular in Europe, anyway, while it fails to offer any surrogate. The function and effects of contingency fees and punitive damages are to provide a risk premium to group representatives, in order to compensate them for the risk they run in favour of group members. European systems scrap these legal institutions (in line with the prohibition of the Recommendation on Collective Redress) without offering anything in exchange in order to tackle the problem of risk premium.

Above, it was argued that it is economically rational for group representatives to enforce group members' claims if all the costs related to the collective action can be shifted on the losing defendant and group representatives are granted a risk premium, i.e. if they win they get a reimbursement higher than their actual costs in order to compensate them for the risk they run when instituting the proceedings.[85] The "American rule" on attorney's fees, contingency fees and punitive damages are meant to be a risk premium (or simply have such an unintended effect). The

---

[79]Commission Recommendation of 11 June 2013 on common principles for injunctive and compensatory collective redress mechanisms in the Member States concerning violations of rights granted under Union Law, para 13.

[80]Id. at para. 29-30. According to the Recommendation, contingency fees can be permitted only exceptionally. ("The Member States that exceptionally allow for contingency fees should provide for appropriate national regulation of those fees in collective redress cases, taking into account in particular the right to full compensation of the members of the claimant party.").

[81]Id. at para 31.

[82]Id. at para 4.

[83]See Grace (2006: 287–288), Waelbroeck et al. (2004: 93–94, 116–17), Leskinen (2011: 98–105).

[84]Wilcox (2009: 7–54).

[85]Nagy (2013: 495–497).

purpose of the "American rule" is to shift some of the risks attached to the plaintiff's or group representative's failure onto the defendant.[86] Super-compensatory damages are clearly risk premiums; punitive and treble damages are meant to incite the plaintiff to litigate through compensating him for the risks he runs because of the litigation.[87] Contingency fees also contain a clear risk premium, because they are presumably higher than the attorney's fees charged in case of no risk[88]; this risk premium is meant to compensate the law firm for the risks it takes over from the client. Albeit jury trials (which appear to issue in higher awards) and generous "pain and suffering" awards are probably not meant to provide a risk premium, this is one of their side-effects.

In US law, it is the provision of generous risk premiums that makes the operation of the US class action so intensive.[89] Ironically, the measures that could make collective litigation effective would move the European regulatory environment towards US law. All the measures the absence of which explained why Europe should not fear the opt-out class action are actually the functional equivalents of a risk premium, even if they are of general application and are not specific to class actions. These ensure that the scheme is effective and wide-spread.[90]

In Europe, the simplest way of compensating group representatives for the risks they assume when enforcing the group's claims would be to grant them a lump sum in excess to their expenses (organizational and ordinary legal costs). Nevertheless, all benefits in excess of compensation would be the functional equivalents of super-compensatory damages. Another solution, introduced, by way of example, in Canada,[91] could be lifting or softening the "loser pays" rule in favour of the group representative; however, again, the risk premium granted to the group representative (and borne by the defendant), whereas lifting one of the hurdles of collective litigation, may create a catalysing factor whose absence is an argument confirming why Europe should not fear the opt-out class action.

All in all, it seems that the effectiveness and widespread use of collective litigation and the potential of abuse and adverse effects are inversely proportional to each other. It would amount to an exaggeration to contend that this is a vicious circle; it is not, it is a trade-off, which does allow fine-tuning. The European legislator or legislators have to find the point of equilibrium where the marginal benefit of effective enforcement equals the marginal cost of abuse and adverse effects. Low risk premiums would encourage collective litigation in good cases but would not be sufficient to be an incentive to take up weak cases. If the risk premium embedded in the US system appears to be excessive in Europe, a lower one should be introduced.

Furthermore, the perils inherent in the risk premium certainly do not refute the proposition that the opt-out class action should not be feared if introduced in the current European regulatory environment. The fact that without an appropriate risk

---

[86] See Gryphon (2011: 569).

[87] Behr (2003: 120–121), Visscher (2009: 224), Koziol (2009: 304).

[88] Nagy (2013: 495–496).

[89] Nagy (2013: 489, 497).

[90] Nagy (2013: 496).

[91] See Kalajdzic et al. (2009: note 29).

premium the intensity of opt-out class actions would not exceed a certain level is not an argument against their introduction. In particular, because the group representative may espouse the collective action for different non-economic reasons; and the limited European experience shows that civil organizations may endeavour to protect the rights of group members, even in case it does not pay out for them to do so.

All in all, the main flaw of European collective actions' treatment of financial incentives is that, in essence, they scrap the risk premium devices of US law, while failing to offer any surrogate.[92] In the absence of an adequate risk premium it will not pay out for group representatives to take up the case; and even if the group representative is a non-profit organization, failing public funding, the entity's expected costs and expected income have to be in balance to make the system sustainable.

4.3.2   Two-Way Cost-Shifting

While in the US, owing to the American rule, group members do not run the risk of becoming responsible for the defendant's attorney's fees, in Europe the principle of two-way cost-shifting prevails. This implies that, even if this principle does not work to the full, group members' financial liability for the legal costs has to be addressed. The general principle of civil procedure requires that someone should be obliged to reimburse the winning party for his legal expenses and there is no reason to deprive the defendants of collective actions of this protection. This obligation may be placed either on individual group members or on the group representative. In opt-in systems both variations are conceivable, as group members join the collective action voluntarily. However, if adopted, opt-out systems entail an additional twist: the strongest argument for the constitutionality of opt-out class actions is that they confer only benefits and no disadvantages on group members; this argument would lose weight if group members were exposed to the risk of being liable for the defendant's legal costs. Hence, the argument for the opt-out scheme's constitutionality may be preserved if group members are freed from all liability and the group representative runs the full risk as to legal costs.

4.3.3   Distrust of Market-Based Mechanisms
in the Enforcement of Public Policy (No Private
Attorney General)

In Europe, class actions are not meant to have a public policy function and serve as a purely compensatory function. A public policy role would be difficult to reconcile with the principle that public policy is the prerogative of the state. The only legitimate purpose of collective actions is to organize the effective enforcement of private law

---

[92]See Geradin (2015: 1096–1099).

claims that would otherwise not be enforced. While this may certainly influence the behavior of undertakings, beyond these side-effects, all public policy aims are left to public law and public authorities. In the same vein, the concept of "private attorney general" is completely alien to European legal systems and for-profit entities' aptness to serve the public interest is normally received with doubt.

As a result, European legislators have been reluctant to vest for-profit private entities with the power to launch collective proceedings. Standing has been normally limited to public entities and non-profit organizations. The general attitude is that financial incentives may give a stimulus that is not reconcilable with the public interest to be protected.

The consequence of this attitude is that in class actions standing is normally conferred on non-profit entities (non-profit organizations, administrative agencies or public prosecutors), which are presumed not to be influenced by inadequate incentives.[93]

4.3.4 European Opt-In Collective Actions and Joinders of Parties

A few EU Member States adopted opt-in systems, ruling out representation without positive authorization. These systems embed the requirement that the group representative, one way or another, has to be explicitly authorized by group members and only those persons are part of the litigation who expressly did so.

Probably the first question that emerges as to the opt-in system is its *raison d'être*: why to have an opt-in scheme if the doctrine of joinder of parties is available for organizing group litigation. The answer lies in the details. A joinder of parties creates a very decentralized system. It is not lead by a group representative, quite the contrary, in a joinder of parties, legally speaking, there is no group representative, though the parties may hire the same attorney. The group is not centralized, group members have equal rights and obligations, they may make individual submissions and their motions may contradict. This makes a traditional joinder of parties unsuitable for mass litigation, in particular in relation to small claims.

The opt-in class action is a centralized joinder of parties that makes mass litigation feasible through the concentration of the representation and the restriction of certain procedural rights of group members (i.e. group members' procedural rights are restricted in comparison to individual litigation). That is, the opt-in class action not only simplifies adherence but also turns the group representative from a marionette into the master of the case.

---

[93] See Fairgrieve and Howells (2009: 400, 407) (The European model regards "public agencies or accredited consumer organizations as a gatekeeper[s].").

4.3.5   Opt-Out Systems and the "Only Benefits" Principle

The taboo of party autonomy has profoundly shaped the European model of collective actions. This entailed that some Member States adopted opt-in schemes, while those who introduced an opt-out system did this along with the "only benefits" principle (i.e. in the opt-out system only benefits may accrue to group members).

According to the "only benefits" principle, the opt-out rule is reconcilable with the constitutional right to party autonomy, because it confers only benefits on group members, so their assent may be presumed. As a corollary, opt-out systems were worked out in a way that group members run no risk as to legal costs and, at times, they are covered by the final judgment's res judicata effects only if they expressly accept it or if that is in their interest.

The French class action yarn demonstrates well how the "only benefits" principle, erected by constitutional considerations, has shaped Europe's paradigm.

France introduced a collective action mechanism for consumers in 2014,[94] which was scrutinized and endorsed by the French Constitutional Council.[95]

The French regulatory regime established a truly unique system (action de groupe à la française), which combines the elements of the opt-out and opt-in models. Even though French law retained the requirement that the consumer needs to adhere through an express declaration, this declaration needs to be submitted only after the judgment has been made, when the consumer turns the award into cash.

The scheme appears to be a de facto opt-out system, although the consumer's right to opt-in is retained and can be exercised after the judgment is made. This is, to some extent, comparable to the opt-out system, since even there, at the end of the day, group members have to act in order to receive their share of the award. At the same time, there is a real difference between the "action de groupe à la française" and opt-out class action. In the former case, the judgment's res judicata effect extends to the group member only if, after having been duly informed, he expressly accepts the judgment and the compensation. If a group member thinks that he can reach a more favourable award, he can enforce his claim individually. However, this seems to be a rather formal difference: it is highly unlikely that in the subsequent individual action the court would reach a different conclusion. Taking into account the rule that the consumer has to step in only in the last phase, after the legal situation has been fixed, and assuming that consumers will go their own way extremely rarely, this system can be reasonably characterized as a de facto opt-out scheme.

The French consumer code (Code de la consommation) establishes a standard group procedure and a simplified procedure. The simplified procedure[96] applies if the identity and the number of the injured consumers are known and they sustained either a harm of the same amount, of the same amount per a given service or of the

---

[94] Act 2014-344 of 17 March 2014 (Loi n° 2014-344 du 17 mars 2014 relative à la consommation publiée au Journal Officiel du 18 mars 2014).

[95] Decision 2014-690 of 13 March 2014 (Le 14 novembre 2014, JORF n°0065 du 18 mars 2014, Texte n°2, Décision n° 2014-690 DC du 13 mars 2014).

[96] Article L423-10 of the French Consumer Code.

same amount for a given period. According to these criteria, the court may establish the defendant's liability and order it to compensate group members directly and individually within the deadline set by the court. The only element which obscures the opt-out nature of this procedure is the rule providing that a consumer can be compensated only after he accepted to be compensated according to the terms of the judgment. The simplified procedure has the strongest opt-out features. From the perspective of res judicata effects, this rule preserves, indeed, the opt-in nature of the procedure, since if the consumer is not content with the judgment, he may take the route of individual litigation. However, notwithstanding the lack of res judicata effects, as noted above, it is highly unrealistic that the court would come to a different conclusion in the subsequent individual litigation. Furthermore, as a matter of fact, the simplified procedure does not make express adherence a pre-condition of the procedure and the judgment. In fact, it does not require much more activity from the consumer than opt-out systems do: the consumer would have to act at the payment or enforcement stage anyway (for example, contact the group representative or the court, initiate the enforcement of the judgment).

The standard procedure follows the same logic.[97] In the first phase, the judge— as a result of the group representative's action—decides on the merits of the case, insofar this is possible. It establishes the defendant's liability, defines the group and establishes the applicable criteria, determines the harms that can be compensated in respect of all consumers or all categories of consumers, including the amount and the elements, which permit the evaluation of the harm. Furthermore, the court establishes the measures that have to be adopted to inform group members and fixes a deadline for adherence. In the second, out-of-court phase, group members are informed and have to decide whether they want to be covered by the judgment. In the ideal case, the defendant pays compensation to them. Should this not happen, the action moves to the third phase, where the court decides on the eventual difficulties of enforcement and on individual cases. Accordingly, the court decides on the merits of the case as early as the first phase. At this stage, consumers' express adherence is not required, and they have to decide whether they want to be compensated. The third stage is left for fine-tuning and individual aspects. Again, the judgment's res judicata effect is conditional on the consumer's acceptance of the judgment. However, this appears to be a rather formal dissimilarity to the opt-out system: as noted above, it seems to be highly unrealistic that the court would come to a different conclusion in the subsequent individual litigation than in the collective action.

It appears that, during the law's constitutional review, it was decisive for the French Constitutional Council that the res judicata effect covers solely those group members who received compensation at the end of the procedure.[98] It seems that the circumstances that only benefits accrue to group members and that the judgment's res judicata effect covers only those group members who assented to it (since compen-

---

[97] Articles L423-3 to L423-9 of the French Consumer Code.

[98] Decision 2014-690 of 13 March 2014 (Le 14 novembre 2014, JORF n°0065 du 18 mars 2014, Texte n°2, Décision n° 2014-690 DC du 13 mars 2014), paras 10 and 16.

sation can be paid only if the group member accepts it) were sufficient to extinguish the possible constitutional concerns.

Before the adoption of the above-mentioned decision, the French Constitutional Council had been referred to as an authority to justify the unconstitutionality of the opt-out system, citing its famous decision of 1989,[99] which dealt with a law that authorized trade unions to launch any action (toutes actions) on behalf of the employee, including claims of unfair dismissal.[100] The French rules adopted in 2014 seem to have gone beyond the constitutional requirements of the decision of 1989, since, although at the end of the procedure, they do require express acceptance from group members, they do not content themselves with tacit adherence.

4.4   Summary

The regulatory and social environments of collective actions differ considerably on the two sides of the Atlantic. Contrary to the US, "entrepreneurial lawyering" is virtually missing in Europe, contingency fees are either prohibited (or available with restrictions) or, even if legal, are normally not available in the market; active client-acquiring and lawyer advertisements are banned or heavily restricted in most EU Member States. The "American rule" and especially one-way cost-shifting, as provided by various American protective statutes, are unknown to European jurisdictions, which traditionally follow the rules of two-way cost-shifting. Super-compensatory damages are not available in Europe, with some narrow and insignificant exceptions in a couple of common law jurisdictions, and the generous US discovery rules have equally no counter-part.

These differences have twofold consequences. First, due to the absence of the above pro-plaintiff incentives, the operation and impact of European collective actions differ considerably from their American ancestor. Second, European legislators have to address quite a few regulatory issues that do not emerge in the US.

Both theoretical analysis and empirical data clearly suggest that the purported negative repercussions of opt-out collective litigation (US class action) would not emerge if this regulatory mechanism were introduced in Europe. The theoretical arguments and the brief account of the empirical evidence in Europe suggest that, whereas the relatively short time that has elapsed since the wide-spread appearance of these mechanisms (both opt-in and opt-out systems) in Europe does not enable us to predict long-term consequences, opt-out collective proceedings would trigger no litigation boom in Europe. This conclusion is underpinned also by the empirical experiments of Australia and Canada, which introduced class actions in a regulatory environment different in some of the relevant aspects from the US.

The transplantation of collective actions into the European legal and social environment raises an array of novel regulatory questions.

---

[99]Décision n° 89-257 DC du 25 juillet 1989.

[100]Id. at para 25.

European legal systems lack the counterparts of US legal institutions that facilitate litigation through the provision of financial incentives (one-way cost-shifting, contingency fees and punitive damages), making litigation finance a crucial regulatory issue. Unfortunately, European collective action laws have failed to settle or even address this problem: while they ruled out the American institutions that stimulate the operation of US class actions, they failed to replace these with appropriate substitutes. Arguably, failing public funding, European class actions have little chance to become effective and self-sustaining, if, one way or another, appropriate financial incentives are not provided for to ensure that the group representative receives a risk premium for running financial risks in the interest of the group. Economically speaking, the group representative's expected income and expected costs cannot be equilibrated in the absence of an appropriate risk premium and, hence, he may be incited to espouse group members' claims, if he is compensated for the risks he runs when engaging in collective litigation.

While in US class action, due to the American rule, group members are not responsible for the defendant's attorney's fees even if the class action fails, in Europe, the principle of two-way cost-shifting prevails, raising—both in opt-in and opt-out systems—the regulatory question of allocation. It is generally accepted that the opt-out scheme's constitutionality may be preserved if group members are freed from all liability and the group representative runs the full risk as to legal costs.

European class actions are not meant to have a public policy function and their role is limited to ensuring a compensatory remedy for group members. As the concept of "private attorney general" is completely alien to European legal systems and the general attitude is that financial incentives may function as an unacceptable stimulus, for-profit entities' aptness to serve the public interest is normally received with doubt. This explains why in Europe standing has been normally limited to public entities and non-profit organizations.

A peculiar element of the architecture of European collective actions is the "only benefits" principle, which prevails in opt-out systems. The strongest argument for "representation without authorization" and against the allegation that opt-out class actions encroach on party autonomy is that only benefits may accrue to group members, so it would be redundant to require express authorization. Hence, these systems were worked out in a way that group members run no risk as to legal costs and they are covered by the final judgment's res judicata effects only if they expressly accept it or if that is in their interest.

References

Alexander JC (2000) An introduction to class action procedure in the United States. Paper presented at "Debates over group litigation in comparative perspective", Geneva, 21–22 July 2000. http://law.duke.edu/grouplit/papers/classactionalexander.pdf. Accessed 20 April 2019

Baert KM, Guindon A (2008) Class proceedings in Ontario: the growing risk of adverse costs awards against representative plaintiffs. Paper presented at the 5th Annual symposium on class actions, Toronto, Canada, 10–11 April 2008

Behr V (2003) Punitive damages in American and German law—tendencies towards approximation of apparently irreconcilable concepts, Chicago-Kent Law Rev 78(1):105–161

Blennerhassett J (2016) A comparative examination of multi-party actions: the case of environmental mass harm. Hart Publishing, Oxford

Bouchard M (1980) L'autorisation d'exercer le recours collectif. Les Cahiers de droit 21(3)-(4):855–959

Branch WK, Montrichard D (2005) Exposing the "litigation blackmail" myth. British Columbia CLE. http://branchmacmaster.squarespace.com/storage/articles/Exposing_the_Litigation_Blackmail_Myth.pdf. Accessed 20 April 2019

Buchner J (2015) Kollektiver Rechtsschutz für Verbraucher in Europa: die grenzüberschreitende Durchsetzung des europäischen Verbraucherrechts bei Bagatellschäden. V&R unipress, Göttingen

Calabresi G, Schwartz KS (2011) The costs of class actions: allocations and collective redress in the US experience. Eur J Law Econ 32(2):169–183

Carbonara E, Parisi F (2012) Rent-seeking and litigation: the hidden virtues of the loser-pays rule. Minnesota Legal Studies Research Paper No. 12–39. http://ssrn.com/abstract=2144800. Accessed 20 April 2019

Chieu T (2010) Class actions in the European Union? Importing lessons learned from the United States' experience into European Community competition law. Cardozo J Int Compar Law 18(1):123–157

Clark SS, Harris C (2001) Multi-plaintiff litigation in Australia: a comparative perspective. Duke J Compar Int Law 11(2):289–320

Delatre JG (2011) Beyond the White Paper: rethinking the Commission's Proposal on private antitrust litigation. Competition Law Rev 8(1):29–58

Ebbing F (2004) Die Gruppeklage: Ein Vorbild für das deutsche Recht. Zeitschrift für vergleichende Rechtswissenschaft 103(1):31–56

Fairgrieve D, Howells G (2009) Collective redress procedures—European debates. Int Compar Law Quarterly 58:379–409

Ferro MS (2015) Collective redress: will Portugal show the way? J Eur Competition Law Practice 6(5):299–300

Friendly HJ (1973) Federal jurisdiction: a general view. Columbia University Press, New York

Geradin D (2015) Collective redress for antitrust damages in the European Union: is this a reality now? George Mason Law Rev 22:1079–1101

Gidi A (2003) Class actions in Brazil—a model for civil law countries. Am J Compar Law 51(2):311–408

Gidi A (2012) The recognition of US class action judgments abroad: the case of Latin America. Brooklyn J of Int Law 37(3):893–965

Gjidara-Decaix S (2010) Les règles de répartition des frais en procédure civile. Revue internationale de droit comparé 62(2):325–360

Gotanda JY (2004) Punitive damages: a comparative analysis. Columbia J Trans Law 42(2):391–444

Grace SM (2006) Strengthening investor confidence in Europe: US-style securities class actions and the acquis communautaire. J Trans Law Policy 15(2):281–304

Gryphon M (2011) Assessing the effects of a "loser pays" rule on the American legal system: an economic analysis and proposal for reform. Rutgers J Law & Public Policy 8(3):567–613

Heffernan L (2003) Comparative common law approaches to multi-party litigation: the American class action procedure. Dublin University law J 25:102–123

Hensler DR (2014) Third-party financing of class action litigation in the United States: will the sky fall? DePaul Law Rev 63(2):499–526

Hodges C (2009) From class actions to collective redress: a revolution in approach to compensation. Civil Justice Quart 28:41–66

Hodges C (2010) Collective redress in Europe: the new model. Civil Justice Quart 29(3):370–395

Isidro MR (2009) Punitive damages from a private international law perspective. In: Koziol H, Wilcox V (eds) Punitive damages: common law and civil law perspectives. Springer, Vienna, pp 237–255

Kalajdzic J (2018) Class actions in Canada: the promise and reality of access to justice. UBC Press, Vancouver

Kalajdzic J, Bogart WA, Matthews I (2009) Canada. Ann Am Acad Polit Social Sci 622(1):41–52

Karlsgodt PG (2012) United States. In: Karlsgodt PG (ed) World class actions: a guide to group and representative actions around the globe. Oxford University Press, Oxford, pp 3–55

Katzarsky A, Georgiev G (2012) Chapter 11: Bulgaria. In: Dodds-Smith I, Brown A (eds) The international comparative legal guide to class & group actions. Global Legal Group, London

Koziol H (2009) Punitive damages: admission into the seventh legal heaven or eternal damnation? Comparative report and conclusions. In: Kozil H, Wilcox V (eds) Punitive damages: common law and civil law perspectives. Springer, Vienna, pp 275–308

Lafond P-C (1998–1999) Le recours collectif: entre la commodité procédurale et la justice sociale. Revue de droit. Université de Sherbrooke 29(1)-(2):3–37

Lafond P-C (2006) La recours collectif, le rôle du juge et sa conception de la justice, impact et evolution. Les Éditions Yvon Blais, Cowansville, Québec

Leskinen C (2011) Collective actions: rethinking funding and national cost rules. Competition Law Rev 8(1):87–121

Mazen N-J (1987) Le recours collectif: réalité québeccoise et projet français. Revue internationale de droit comparé 39(2):373–411

Morabito V (2009a) Australia. The ANNALS of the American Academy of political and social science 622(1):320–327

Morabito V (2009b) An empirical study of Australia's class action regimes: first report. Global class actions exchange. http://globalclassactions.stanford.edu/sites/default/files/documents/Australia_Empirical_Morabito_2009_Dec.pdf. Accessed 20 April 2019

Nagy CI (2013) Comparative collective redress from a law and economics perspective: without risk there is no reward! Columbia J Eur Law 19(3):469–498

Nagy CI (2015) The European collective redress debate after the European Commission's Recommendation: one step forward, two steps back? Maastricht J Eur Compar Law 22(4):530–552

Neumann K-A, Magnusson LW (2011) Pour une class-action européenne dans le droit de la concurrence. Revue québécoise de droit international 24(2):149–181

Parisi F, Cenini M (2008) Punitive damages and class actions. Minnesota Legal Studies Research Paper No. 08–38. http://ssrn.com/abstract=1264511. Accessed 20 April 2019

Piñeiro LC (2007) La tipicidad de las acciones colectivasen el ordenamiento jurídico español. Justicia: revista de derecho procesal 27(3)-(4):63–65

Posner RA (1973) An economic approach to legal procedure and judicial administration. J Legal Stud 2(2):399–458

Posner RA (2001) Antitrust in the new economy. Antitrust Law J 68(3):925–943

Rossi L, Ferro MS (2013) Private enforcement of competition law in Portugal (II): actio popularis—facts, fictions and dreams. Revista de Concorrência e Regulação 4(1):35–87

Russell TL (2010) Exporting class actions to the European Union. Boston Univ Int Law J 28:141–180

Rustada ML (2005) The closing of punitive damages' iron cage. Loyola of Los Angeles Law Rev 38:1297–1420

Sebok JA (2007) Punitive damages: from myth to theory. Iowa Law Rev 92(3):957–1036

Sebok JA (2009) Punitive damages in the United States. In: Koziol H, Wilcox V (eds) Punitive damages: common law and civil law perspectives. Springer, Vienna, pp 155–196

Smithka Ch (2009) From Budapest to Berlin: how implementing class action lawsuits in the European Union would increase competition and strengthen consumer confidence. Wisconsin Int Law J 27:173–193

Stephen FH, Love JH (2000) Regulation of the legal profession. In: Boudewijn B, de Geest G (eds) Encyclopedia of law and economics, vol 3. Edward Elgar Publishing, Cheltenham

Stier B, Tzankova I (2016) The culture of collective litigation: a comparative analysis. In: Hensler DR, Christopher Hodges C, Tzankova I (eds) Class actions in context: how culture, economics and politics shape collective litigation. Edward Elgar Publishing, Cheltenham

Strong SI (2012) Regulatory litigation in the European Union: does the U.S. class action have a new analogue? Notre Dame Law Rev 88:899–971

Stuyck J et al (2007) An analysis and evaluation of alternative means of consumer redress other than redress through ordinary judicial proceedings: final report. http://www.eurofinas.org/uploads/documents/policies/OTHER%20POLICY%20ISSUES/comparative_report_en.pdf. Accessed 20 April 2019

Udvary S (2013) The advantages and disadvantages of class action. Iustum Aequum Salutare 9(1):67–82

Visscher LT (2009) Economic analysis of punitive damages. In: Koziol H, Wilcox V (eds) Punitive damages: common law and civil law perspectives. Springer, Vienna, pp 219–236

Voet S (2016) The crux of the matter: funding and financing collective redress mechanisms. In: Hess B, Bergström M, Storskrubb E (eds) EU civil justice: current issues and future outlook. Hart Publishing, Oxford, pp 201–222

Waelbroeck D, Slater D, Even-Shoshan G (2004) Comparative report. In: Study on the conditions of claims for damages in case of infringement of EC competition rules. Ashurst. http://ec.europa.eu/competition/antitrust/actionsdamages/comparative_report_clean_en.pdf. Accessed 20 April 2019

Watson GD (2001) Class actions: the Canadian experience. Duke J Int and Compar Law 11:269–287

Wegen G, Sherer J (1993) Germany: Federal Court of Justice decision concerning the recognition and enforcement of US judgments awarding punitive damages [June 4, 1992]. Int Legal Mater 32:1320–1346

Weinstein JB (1997) Some reflections on United States group actions. Am J Compar Law 45(4):833–837

Wilcox V (2009) Punitive damages in England. In: Koziol H, Wilcox V (eds) Punitive damages: common law and civil law perspectives. Springer, Vienna, pp 7–53

Chapter 5
European Models of Collective Actions

Aside from some general legal requirements, EU law contains no "federal" legal framework for Member States' collective action regimes. Member States have procedural autonomy in the application of EU law, that is, they are free to determine the structure and way of application and enforcement,[1] with the proviso that national law must not discriminate between the application of EU and domestic law (principle of equivalence)[2] and "must not be so framed as to make it virtually impossible or excessively difficult to obtain reparation (principle of effectiveness)."[3]

In 2013, the European Commission adopted a Recommendation on Collective Redress,[4] a non-binding legal instrument,[5] proposing that Member States adopt collective redress mechanisms for violations of EU law. Although it may certainly have an impact on Member State laws,[6] as noted above, contrary to a directive, the

---

[1] See e.g. Case 51-54/71 *International Fruit Company*, [1971] ECR 1107, ECLI:EU:C:1971:128, paras 3 and 4.

[2] See e.g. Case 33/76, *Rewe-Zentralfinanz eG and Rewe-Zentral AG v Landwirtschaftskammer für das Saarland*, [1976] ECR 1989, ECLI:EU:C:1976:188, para 5.

[3] See e.g. Case C-261/95 *Rosalba Palmisani v Istituto nazionale della previdenza sociale* (*INPS*), [1997] ECR I-4025, ECLI:EU:C:1997:351, para 27.

[4] For an analysis of the Recommendation, see Piñeiro (2013), Szalai (2014), Stadler (2015: 61) and Nagy (2015: 530).

[5] Article 288 TFEU.

[6] In fact, the Recommendation's impact on positive law in the Member States has been rather slight, see Commission Report on the implementation of the Commission Recommendation of 11 June 2013 on common principles for injunctive and compensatory collective redress mechanisms in the Member States concerning violations of rights granted under Union law (2013/396/EU), COM(2018) 40 final, p 20. ("As far as the transition into legislation is concerned, the analysis of the legislative developments in Member States as well as the evidence provided demonstrate that there has been a rather limited follow-up to the Recommendation. The availability of collective redress mechanisms as well as the implementation of safeguards against the potential abuse of such mechanisms is still very unevenly distributed across the EU. The impact of the Recommendation is visible in the two Member States where new legislation was adopted after its adoption (BE and LT) as well as in SI where new legislation is pending, and to a certain extent in the Member States that changed their legislation after 2013 (FR and UK).")

© The Author(s) 2019
C. I. Nagy, *Collective Actions in Europe*,
SpringerBriefs in Law, https://doi.org/10.1007/978-3-030-24222-0_5

Recommendation creates no framework for national regulation. Its significance and potential impact has to be assessed accordingly.

The Recommendation follows a conservative approach. It suggests restricting group representation to non-profit entities and public authorities.[7] Furthermore, it expresses a strong preference towards the opt-in system, recommending that only those group members should be involved in the collective action who expressly assented to it.[8] The Recommendation does not ban the opt-out scheme outright but leaves open a gate, even if a small one, to such mechanisms: "[a]ny exception to [the opt-in] principle, by law or by court order, should be duly justified by reasons of sound administration of justice."[9]

The Recommendation introduces safeguards in order to obviate the incentives to abuse the mechanism of collective actions: it makes the use of the "loser pays" principle mandatory,[10] excludes, at least in principle, contingency fees[11] and prohibits punitive damages.[12]

The above European federal framework may change considerably in the foreseeable future. In April 2018, the Commission proposed the adoption of a consumer collective action scheme (termed "representative action").[13] The proposed directive is in accordance with the common principles of European collective action laws: it has a sectoral approach (consumer protection), rigorous pre-conditions, confers standing on qualified representative entities, maintains the "loser pays rule" and rules out financial incentives, such as contingency fees and punitive damages. It evades the dilemma of opt-in and opt-out through leaving the choice to Member States.[14] Given that most national collective action schemes already comply with these requirements,

---

[7]Recommendation on Collective Redress, paras 4–7.

[8]Trstenjak (2015: 689).

[9]Recommendation on Collective Redress, para 21. ("The claimant party should be formed on the basis of express consent of the natural or legal persons claiming to have been harmed ('opt-in' principle). Any exception to this principle, by law or by court order, should be duly justified by reasons of sound administration of justice.")

[10]Recommendation on Collective Redress, para 13.

[11]Recommendation on Collective Redress, paras 29–30. According to the Recommendation, contingency fees can be permitted only exceptionally. ("The Member States that exceptionally allow for contingency fees should provide for appropriate national regulation of those fees in collective redress cases, taking into account in particular the right to full compensation of the members of the claimant party.")

[12]Recommendation on Collective Redress, para 31.

[13]Proposal for a Directive on representative actions for the protection of the collective interests of consumers, and repealing Directive 2009/22/EC, COM(2018) 184 final. See European Parliament legislative resolution of 26 March 2019 on the proposal for a directive of the European Parliament and of the Council on representative actions for the protection of the collective interests of consumers, and repealing Directive 2009/22/EC (COM(2018)0184–C8-0149/2018–2018/0089(COD)).

[14]Article 6.

the directive is supposed to entail no landslide conceptual reform. Instead, its major virtue is expected to be the introduction of consumer collective action in one third of the Member States where this meachanism is still not available at all.

This chapter gives a transsystemic overview of the European national solutions and schemes along the key issues of class actions.[15] It presents the European landscape, the opt-in and opt-out systems and their main features, the purview of collective action laws featuring a precautious, step-by-step evolution, the pre-requisites of collective actions and certification, the rules on standing and adequate representation, the status of group members, their liability for legal costs and the res judicata effect in opt-in proceedings, the operation of the "only benefits" principle in opt-out proceedings and its impact on the status of group members, and the enforcement of judgments in collective actions.

5.1 The European Landscape: To Opt in or to Opt Out?

In Europe, the history of collective actions started roughly three decades ago.[16] Collective action law gained a foothold in the mid-1990s. Aside from the English representative action, a doctrine rooted in common law but rarely used in practice,[17] class action legislation first appeared in the Hispanic peninsula (Spain, 1984; Portugal, 1995), in Greece in consumer protection law (1994) and in Hungary in the field of competition law (1996). Interestingly, all these systems were based on the opt-out principle and, even more interestingly, they proved to be less effective than one would expect from an opt-out scheme, and way less effective than US class actions. These were followed by the introduction of various opt-in and opt-out schemes. Today, 17 out of 28 Member States provide for collective actions[18] and 10 out of them have

---

[15]For a general typology, see Hensler (2017: 971–979).

[16]See Fairgrieve and Howells (2009: 383–401).

[17]Sherman (2002: 402).

[18]Commission's Report on the implementation of the Recommendation on Collective Redress says that "Compensatory collective redress is available in 19 Member States (AT, BE, BG, DE, DK, FI, FR, EL, HU, IT, LT, MT, NL, PL, PT, RO, ES, SE, UK)." Commission Report on the implementation of the Commission Recommendation of 11 June 2013 on common principles for injunctive and compensatory collective redress mechanisms in the Member States concerning violations of rights granted under Union law (2013/396/EU), COM(2018) 40 final, p 3. However, somewhat misleadingly, it also lists Member States where there is admittedly no "legislation on compensatory relief" but "collective actions are carried out on the basis of the assignment of claims or the joinder of cases."

a system based, at least partially, on the opt-out principle (Belgium,[19] Bulgaria,[20] Denmark,[21] France,[22] Greece,[23] Hungary,[24] Portugal,[25] Slovenia,[26] Spain,[27] and the

---

[19]The Belgian system leaves it to the judge to decide whether the action should be conducted according to the opt-in or the opt-out model. Law Inserting a Title 2 on 'Collective Compensation Action' in Book XVII 'Special Jurisdictional Procedures' of the Code of Economic Law, 28 March 2014, Moniteur Belge (M.B.) (Official Gazette of Belgium (29 March 2014) (Loi portant insertion d'un titre 2 «De l'action en réparation collective» au livre XVII «Procédures juridictionnelles particulières» du Code de droit économique et portant insertion des définitions propres au livre XVII dans le livre 1er du Code de droit économique) and Section XVII.38 in conjunction with Section I.21 of the Belgian Code of Economic Law.

[20]Chapter 33, Sections 379-388 of the Bulgarian Code of Civil Procedure, for an English version of the statutory text, see https://kenarova.com/law/Code%20of%20Civil%20Procedure.pdf. Accessed 20 April 2019. See Katzarsky and Georgiev (2012: 64).

[21]Sections 254a–254e of the Administration of Justice Act.

[22]In France, de facto opt-out class actions were first introduced in the field of consumer protection in 2014, Loi n° 2014-344 du 17 mars 2014 relative à la consommation et Décr. n° 2014-1081 du 24 sept. 2014 relatif à l'action de groupe en matière de consommation, followed by the health care sector in January 2016, Loi n° 2016-41 du 26 janv. 2016 de modernisation de notre système de santé et Décr. n° 2016-1249 du 26 sept. 2016 relatif à l'action de groupe en matière de santé. In November 2016, a general framework was created in France for group actions. Loi n° 2016-1547 du 18 novembre 2016 de modernisation de la justice du XXIe siècle, JORF n° 0269 du 19 novembre 2016 texte n° 1. The new regime extended the purview of the mechanism to discrimination, environmental protection, personal data and health care matters, inserting Sections 826-2–826-24 into the French Code of Civil Procedure.

[23]Articles 10(16)-(29) of Law 2251/1994 on Consumers' Protection.

[24]Section 92 of Hungarian Competition Act (1996. évi LVII. törvény a tisztességtelen piaci magatartás és a versenykorlátozás tilalmáról); Sections 38-38/A of Hungarian Consumer Protection Act (Act CLV of 1997) (1997. évi CLV. törvény a fogyasztóvédelemről); Sections 580-591 of the new Hungarian Code of Civil Procedure effective as from 1 January 2018 (Act CXXX of 2016 on the Code of Civil Procedure, in Hungarian: 2016. évi CXXX. törvény a polgári perrendtartásról).

[25]Law 83/95 on the Acção Popular. See Rossi and Ferro (2013: 46–64) and Ferro (2015: 299–300).

[26]Law on Collective Actions (Zakon o kolektivnih tožbah—ZkolT), Official Journal of the Republic of Slovenia No. 55/2017.

[27]See Section 20 of Law 26/1984 of 19 July on Consumer Protection (Ley para la defensa de los consumidores y usuarios), now Section 24 of Royal Legislative Decree 1/2007 of 16 November,

United Kingdom[28]).[29] Accordingly, more than half of the Member States have sanctioned the introduction of collective actions and from those who did, more than half chose, to some extent, the opt-out system and only less than half stuck fully to the more conservative opt-in principle (Finland,[30] Germany,[31] Italy,[32] Lithuania,[33] Malta,[34] Poland[35] and Sweden[36]).

A couple of states adopted mechanisms that may resemble collective actions but cannot be regarded as a means of collective civil litigation (Fig. 5.1). For reasons advanced above in Sect. 4.3.4, traditional procedural institutions (joinder of parties and assignment of claims) cannot be considered a form of collective action, although they are at times used for the purpose of collective litigation in a couple of Member States (e.g. Austria and the Netherlands). Virtually every single Member State law provides for this possibility and in 11 Member States (Austria, Croatia, Cyprus, Czech Republic, Estonia, Ireland, Latvia, Luxembourg, the Netherlands, Romania, Slovakia), beyond these legal instituions, no special procedural scheme is available

---

which issued a consolidated text on the Law on Consumer Protection and other supplementary laws (Texto refundido de la Ley General para la Defensa de los Consumidores y Usuarios y otras leyes complementarias). This provision was later on inserted in almost every special consumer law issued by the Spanish legislator. See Piñeiro (2007) 63–65. The Spanish Civil Procedure Act of 2000 is, though, the first attempt to systematize the rules of collective proceedings (Articles 6, 11, 15, 15bis, 221, 222(2), 256(1)(6), 519).

[28] See e.g. Sections 18-19 of the 2002 Enterprise Act, which were inserted in Sections 47/A-47/D of the 1998 Competition Act. See also Group Litigation Orders in Sections 19.10. and 19.11. of the Civil Procedure Rules.

[29] *Contra* Commission Report on the implementation of the Commission Recommendation of 11 June 2013 on common principles for injunctive and compensatory collective redress mechanisms in the Member States concerning violations of rights granted under Union law (2013/396/EU), COM(2018) 40 final, p 13. (Considering French, Hungarian and Spanish law to contain an opt-in system.)

[30] Act 444/2007 on Group Actions (Ryhmäkannelaki).

[31] Gesetz zur Einführung einer zivilprozessualen Musterfeststellungsklage (MuFKlaG k.a.Abk.). G. v. 12.07.2018 BGBl. I S. 1151 (Nr. 26).

[32] See Law No 99 of 23 July 2009.

[33] Chapter XXIV[1], Section 441[1–17] of the Lithuanian Code of Civil Procedure with the latest amendment on 8 November 2016 No. XII-2751.

[34] Act VI of 2012. See http://www.justiceservices.gov.mt/DownloadDocument.aspx?app=lom& itemid=11910&l=1. Accessed 20 April 2019.

[35] Act of 17 December 2009 on Pursuing Claims in Group Proceedings (Ustawa z dnia 17 grudnia 2009 r. o dochodzeniu roszczeń w postępowaniu grupowym), Journal of Laws from 2010, No. 7, item 44. The law was comprehensively amended by Act of 7 April 2017 amending different laws in order to facilitate recovery of debts—(Ustawa z dnia 7 kwietnia 2017 r. o zmianie niektórych ustaw w celu ułatwienia dochodzenia wierzytelności), published in Dziennik Ustaw (Journal of Laws) of 2017, item 933. The amendments entered into force on 1 June 2017.

[36] Group Proceedings Act, SFS 2002: 599.

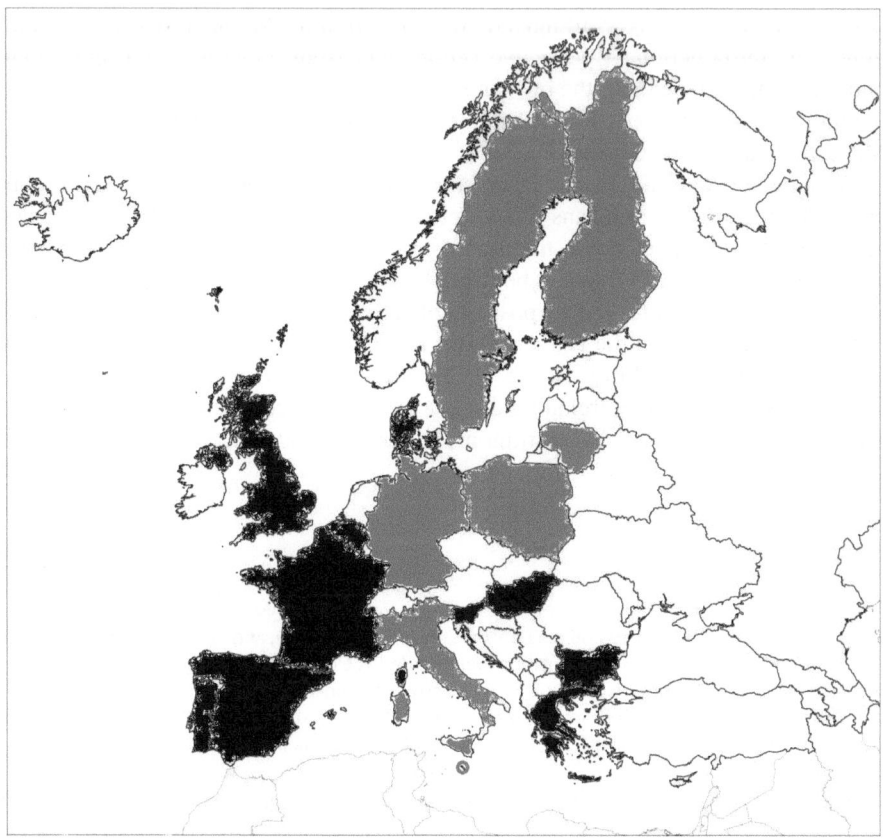

Fig. 5.1 The European collective action landscape (grey: solely opt-in collective actions are available, black: opt-out collective actions are available)

for collective monetary claims, even though collective proceedings are available for injunctions and declaratory judgments.[37]

Although usually listed among Europe's opt-out collective proceedings, the Dutch collective settlement is not considered to be a collective action, as it merely provides a framework for cases where the defendant concedes liability and is ready to settle. In 2005, the Netherlands adopted the Act on Collective Settlement of Mass Damages (Wet collectieve afwikkeling massaschade),[38] which is applicable (as its name suggests) solely to settlements and, accordingly, cannot be used to claim recovery. The group is represented by a social organization, which may conclude a settlement

---

[37] See British Institute of International and Comparative Law (2017: 10) and European Parliament, Policy Department for Citizens' Rights and Constitutional Affairs, Directorate General for Internal Policies of the Union (2018: 18).

[38] The Act entered into force on 27 July 2005. For a comprehensive analysis on the Act, see Krans (2014) and Bosters (2017: 47–59).

with the tortfeasor; the settlement has to be approved by the court.[39] Group members may opt-out from the settlement within three months.

Likewise, regimes providing for the disgorgement of illicitly obtained proceeds for the public budget are not regarded as collective actions, as they are not meant to compensate the victims. For instance, German law, in the field of antitrust and unfair competition law, provides for a disgorgement procedure where wrongdoers may be enjoined to surrender the illicitly acquired economic benefits, however, the proceeds, instead of the victims, go to the federal budget. In the field of unfair competition law, certain associations may sue for monetary relief equal to the illicit profits, less the sums the wrongdoer paid because of the violation, to third parties or the state. The association may enforce the creaming-off claim without the express authorization of group members, however, the money awarded does not go to the victims but to the central budget.[40] Similar rules are embedded in the German Antitrust Law, which applies in cases where the German Federal Competition Office (Bundeskartellamt) adopted no measure to cream off the illicit profits and provides that the Office shall reimburse the associations for their costs up-to the payments they secured for the federal budget.[41] Accordingly, the creaming-off mechanism's function is not to secure a private remedy for the injured parties but to supplement public enforcement.[42]

In same vein, judicial mechanisms that help to coordinate the adjudication of parallel individual proceedings after they have been launched are not considered to be collective actions, as they are not related to access to justice and are not aimed at enhancing the effectiveness of law. For instance, in 2005, Germany introduced a statutory test-case mechanism in capital market law for investor claims.[43] However, this mechanism does not unite individual claims to be submitted and enforced jointly but streamlines individual actions already launched. It creates a possibility to suspend individual actions and to have the common legal and factual issues decided by a single court.

As noted above, while Europe is generally considered to feature the opt-in scheme, this observation is only partially valid. On the one hand, it is true that representation without authorization is generally disapproved taking into account that in 40% of the Member States solely traditional joinder of parties and assignment of claims are

---

[39]The approval of these settlements comes under the competence of the Court of Appeals in Amsterdam.

[40]Section 10 of the German Act against Unfair Competition (Gesetz gegen den unlauteren Wettbewerb—UWG), Gesetz gegen den unlauteren Wettbewerb in der Fassung der Bekanntmachung vom 3. März 2010 (BGBl. I S. 254), last amended through Section 4 of Gesetz vom 17. Februar 2016 (BGBl. I S. 233).

[41]Section 34a of the German Act against Restrictions of Competition (Gesetz gegen Wettbewerbsbeschränkungen—GWB), Gesetz gegen Wettbewerbsbeschränkungen in der Fassung der Bekanntmachung vom 26. Juni 2013 (BGBl. I S. 1750, 3245), last amended through Section 5 of Gesetz vom 13. Oktober 2016 (BGBl. I S. 2258).

[42]Cf. Stadler (2009: 117).

[43]Law on Model Proceedings in Capital Market Disputes (Gesetz über Musterverfahren in kapitalmarktrechtlichen Streitigkeiten—KapMuG), adopted on August 16, 2005 (BGBl. I S. 2437). See Halfmeier and Feess (2012), Steinberger (2016: 44–132) and Bosters (2017: 27–34).

available as a means to bring collective claims to court. On the other hand, from the 17 Member States which created a special regime for collective litigation, only 7 stuck fully to the opt-in principle.

The 2002 Swedish Act on Group Proceedings[44] is one of the first comprehensive national codifications of collective actions that covered the whole spectrum of civil claims (and not only specific sectors or branches of law).[45] The Swedish Act entered into force on 1 January 2003. Although it adopts an opt-in system, the available statistical data suggests that the Swedish Group Proceedings Act is relatively effective: 17 group proceedings were initiated until the beginning of 2014 (that is, in the first 12 years of the law).[46] These matters include the enforcement of air passengers' rights, claims by insurance holders, a procedure against the Swedish state for violating EU law, overcharges concerning electricity supply (violation of fixed universal service prices).[47]

The Finnish parliament adopted the Act on Collective Proceedings in February 2007, after 15 years of social debate[48]; the Act came into force on 1 October 2007.[49] The central feature of the Finnish system is that is creates an opt-in system[50] empowering exclusively the Consumer Ombudsman to institute a collective action[51] in matters coming under its competence (consumer matters).[52] Until recently, there has been no proceedings instituted on the basis of the Finnish Act[53]; this may be explained with the opt-in rule and with the fact that collective actions may be launched exclusively by the Consumer Ombudsman.[54] Of course, the lack of cases does not necessarily mean that the Finnish Act has been devoid of impact on the behavior of enterprises.[55]

---

[44]Group Proceedings Act, SFS 2002:599. For the non-official translation of the Act, see https://www.government.se/government-policy/judicial-system/group-proceedings-act/ and http://www.courdecassation.fr/IMG/File/loi_suedoise_swedish_law_eng.pdf. Accessed 20 April 2019. The Act entered into force on 1 January 2003. For a comprehensive analysis of the draft version, see Lindblom (1997: 824–830), Nordh (2001: 395–402), Lindblom (2007) and Persson (2012).

[45]Sections 1-2 of the Swedish Act on Group Proceedings.

[46]Ervo (2016: 188). See also Ervo et al. (Unknown).

[47]Lindblom (2008: 2–7) (reporting 12 cases.). Cf. Persson (2008: 17) (reporting 11 cases).

[48]Act 444/2007 on Class Actions (Ryhmäkannelaki), for an unofficial English translation of the Act, see http://www.finlex.fi/fi/laki/kaannokset/2007/en20070444.pdf. Accessed 20 April 2019. For an analysis on the Act, see Viitanen (2007).

[49]Section 19 of the Finnish Act on Class Action.

[50]Section 8(1) of the Finnish Act on Class Action.

[51]Section 4 of the Finnish Act on Class Action.

[52]The Act is not applicable to capital market matters.

[53]Ervo (2016: 189) and Kiurunen (2012: 226).

[54]Välimäki (2007) and Viitanen (2008: 2).

[55]It may be used as a leverage to compel a settlement. See "Caruna and the Consumer Ombudsman reached a negotiated solution—no need for a class action lawsuit, but changes in the Electricity Market Act still in the agenda". http://www.hankintajuristit.fi/caruna-and-the-consumer-ombudsman-reached-a-negotiated-solution-no-need-for-a-class-action-lawsuit-but-changes-in-the-electricity-market-act-still-in-the-agenda/. Accessed 20 April 2019.

The Italian legislator enacted a law on collective actions in December 2007 by inserting Section 140bis in the Italian Consumer Code.[56] These rules were, nevertheless, replaced by a new Section 140bis,[57] which entered into force on 1 January 2010.[58] Contrary to the rules of 2007, which referred to the "collective interests" of group members, according to the rules of 2009, the collective action aims to protect the "individual interests" of group members. In 2012, one of the pre-requisites of collective action was softened: as from 25 March 2012, it suffices if the rights of group members are "homogeneous", they do not have to be "identical" anymore.[59] The Italian class action may be used only for pursuing consumer claims arising from specific cases: standard contractual terms and conditions, defective products and services, unfair commercial practices and anticompetitive conducts.[60] According to publicly available sources, 58 class actions had been launched under this provision until January 2016, although a considerable part of them was declared inadmissible and the vast majority of them is pending.[61]

Poland introduced collective actions in 2009 (Act on Pursuing Claims in Group Proceedings). These rules went into effect on 19 July 2010.[62] The Act underwent significant changes in 2017,[63] which entered into force on 1 June 2017. The regime initially applied to consumer law, product and tort liability (with the exception of the protection of personal interests). In 2017, it was extended to claims resulting from the non-performance or undue performance of an obligation, unjust enrichment and certain infringements of personal interests (bodily injury or health disorder).[64] The Act follows the opt-in principle.[65] Members may join the group after the court certifies it.[66] Standing is conferred on class members and the regional consumer

---

[56] Act 244 of 24 December 2007. For a comprehensive analysis of the Italian legislation, see Caponi (2011a: 61), Caponi (2011b) and Ernesto and Fernando (2012).

[57] Act 99 of 23 July 2009. http://www.tedioli.com/Italian_class_action_text_english_version.pdf. Accessed 20 April 2019.

[58] In respect of the Italian legislation, see Silvestri (2007a, b, 2008).

[59] Law no. 27 dated 24 March 2012 under the heading "Rules to make class actions effective".

[60] Section 140bis(2) of the Italian Consumer Code; Principe (2012). Recently, in *Adusbef v Monte dei Paschi di Siena*, the court of appeals of Florence held that retail investors are not consumers and, hence, are not covered by the Italian class action legislation. Afferni (2016: 82, 85).

[61] See the overview provided at http://www.osservatorioantitrust.eu/it/azioni-di-classe-incardinate-nei-tribunali-italiani/. Accessed 20 April 2019. For more information on the case-law, see http://www.collectiveredress.org/collective-redress/reports/italy/caselaw. Accessed 20 April 2019.

[62] Act of 17 December 2009 on Pursuing Claims in Group Proceedings (Ustawa z dnia 17 grudnia 2009 r. o dochodzeniu roszczeń w postępowaniu grupowym). Journal of Laws from 2010, No. 7, item 44.

[63] Act of 7 April 2017 amending different laws in order to facilitate recovery of debts—(Ustawa z dnia 7 kwietnia 2017 r. o zmianie niektórych ustaw w celu ułatwienia dochodzenia wierzytelności), published in Dziennik Ustaw (Journal of Laws) of 2017, item 933.

[64] Sections 1(2) and 1(2)(a)–(b) of the Polish Act on Pursuing Claims in Group Proceedings.

[65] Sections 6(2), 11 and 13(2) of the Polish Act on Pursuing Claims in Group Proceedings.

[66] Section 11(1) of the Polish Act on Pursuing Claims in Group Proceedings.

ombudsman (a public body).[67] Notwithstanding the opt-in rule, the Polish system has produced numerous cases.[68]

Malta introduced opt-in collective actions in 2012 covering the violations of consumer protection, competition and product safety law.[69] Group members may join the action within the deadline specified by the court.[70] It appears that so far two cases have been launched.[71]

Lithuania introduced collective actions in 2015.[72] The regime was inserted into the Lithuanian Code of Civil Procedure[73] (articles 441^1 to article 441^{17}).[74] The act introduced an opt-in scheme of general application having a horizontal approach. So far the Lithuanian rules have been applied in a handful of cases.[75]

Germany introduced a "model declaratory claim" (Musterfeststellungsklage) in 2018, which was inserted as Book 6 (Sections 606-614) in the Code of Civil Procedure (Zivilprozessordnung).[76] The collective action, which entered into force on 1 November 2018, created an opt-in scheme for consumer matters. As a peculiar feature of the Germany system, courts have no power to award damages but may enter a declaratory judgment as to the pre-conditions of liability (they may establish that the claim's or legal relationship's factual and legal pre-conditions exist or do not exist).[77] Group members may seek monetary relief, on an individual basis, after the pre-conditions of the defendant's liability have been established. The final declaratory judgment is binding on courts in matters between the defendant and those consumers who opted in, provided these have the same aim and concern the same fact pattern as the collective declaratory judgment.[78] Since the law's very recent entry into force, the

---

[67] Section 4(2) of the Polish Act on Pursuing Claims in Group Proceedings.

[68] See the statistics of the Polish Ministry of Justice for the period between 2010 and 2016, Pozwy zbiorowe w latach 2010–2016, at https://isws.ms.gov.pl/pl/baza-statystyczna/opracowania-wieloletnie/download,2853,32.html. Accessed on 20 April 2019.

[69] Articles 3-4 and Schedule A of the Maltese Collective Proceedings Act.

[70] Articles 2 (definition of represented person), 7-8 and 18 of the Maltese Collective Proceedings Act.

[71] British Institute of International and Comparative Law (2017) 217.

[72] It has to be noted that group actions were theoretically available also before 2015. Section 49(6) of the Lithuanian Code of Civil Procedure, introduced in 2003, made provision for group actions in case it was necessary to protect the public interest. However, as confirmed by ruling Nr. 2-492/2009 of the Court of Appeal of Lithuania, this provision could not be put into practice as it was not accompanied by an effective implementation mechanism. New Chapter XXIV¹ on Collective Redress was inserted into the Code of Civil Procedure which came into effect on 1 January 2015 and repealed Section 49(6). See Juška (Unknown).

[73] Section 441^{1-17} of the Lithuanian Code of Civil Procedure.

[74] For an English version of the 2015 Lithuanian Class Action Act see Renata Juzikienè's unofficial translation at http://globalclassactions.stanford.edu/sites/default/files/documents/Class_Action_Lithuania.pdf. Accessed 20 April 2019. In the following, the quotes from the Lithuanian legislation refer to the foregoing translation.

[75] See Juška (Unknown).

[76] See Halfmeier (2017) and Schäfer (2018).

[77] Section 606(1) of the German Code of Civil Procedure.

[78] Section 613(1) of the German Code of Civil Procedure.

institution of three cases has been published[79]; the first "model declaratory claim" (emerging from Volkswagen's notorious diesel emissions scandal)[80] was submitted on the very day when the rules entered into force.

In the EU, there are 10 Member States which have sanctioned (at least partially) an opt-out scheme.

Four of these combine the opt-in and the opt-out rule and leave it to the judge to decide under which scheme to carry out the collective action.[81]

The Danish rules on collective action are applicable to proceedings instituted as from 1 January 2008.[82] It is up to the court to decide whether to carry out the action in the opt-in or the opt-out scheme. However, the value of this flexibility is significantly reduced by the fact that the opt-out scheme can be used only if the group representative is an administrative agency.[83] The court decides for the opt-out pattern if the claims' individual enforcement is not feasible due to their low monetary value and it may be assumed that the opt-in pattern would not be appropriate for managing the claims. According to the *travaux préparatoir*, the monetary value of the claim is low if it does not involve more than DKK 2000 (approximately € 270).[84] If the court adopts the opt-out pattern, a deadline is set for group members to abandon the collective action. Until recently, there has been nine cases launched on the basis of the Danish Act on Class Action.[85]

In the same vein, in Belgium,[86] it is up to the court's discretion whether to certify the collective action under the opt-in or the opt-out scheme.[87] However, group members residing habitually or having their principal place of business outside Belgium are covered only if they opt in.[88] Furthermore, only the opt-in scheme may be used in case of physical and moral damages.[89]

---

[79] See the registry of "model declaratory claim" cases (Register für Musterfeststellungsklagen) of the German federal ministry of justice at https://www.bundesjustizamt.de/DE/Themen/Buergerdienste/Klageregister/Allgemeines_node.html. Accessed on 20 April 2019.

[80] Weimann (2018: 38). Interestingly, while facing technical hurdles in Germany, in the diesel emissions case an opt-out collective action was launched in Belgium. Staudt (2019: 157).

[81] For a scholarly proposal suggesting that the choice between the opt-in and the opt-out scheme should be made dependent on the sum of the claims, see Neumann and Magnusson (2011: 169–170).

[82] For an English summary of the Danish legislation, see Werlauff (2008).

[83] Although it is not an EU Member State, it is noteworthy that the Norwegian rules on collective actions entered into force on the same day as their Danish counter-parts. The rules on collective proceedings were included in Chapter 35 of the Dispute Act. For an English translation of the Norwegian rules, see http://globalclassactions.stanford.edu/sites/default/files/documents/Norway_Legislation.pdf. Accessed 20 April 2019. The two systems follow roughly the same model: both combine the opt-in and the opt-out scheme and leave the choice between the two to the court.

[84] Møgelvang-Hansen (2008: 5) and Nielsen and Linhart (2012: 236).

[85] See Ervo (2016: 189).

[86] See Laffineur and Renier (2016).

[87] For an overview, see Paris (2015: 23–24).

[88] Sections XVII.38 and XVII.43 of the Belgian Code on Economic Law (Code de droit économique).

[89] Section XVII.43 3° of the Belgian Code on Economic Law.

In the United Kingdom, due to a mechanism introduced in 2015,[90] opt-out class actions are available in competition matters and it is up to the Competition Appeal Tribunal (CAT) to decide whether the procedure will be carried out in the opt-in or the opt-out scheme.[91] It is worthy of note that class members domiciled outside the United Kingdom have to opt-in, even if the CAT chose the opt-out scheme for the case. The Competition Act does not set out the factors the CAT has to take into account when exercising its discretion, however, the Competition Appeal Tribunal Rules of 2015 list two considerations: "the strength of the claims" and "whether it is practicable for the proceedings to be brought as opt-in collective proceedings, having regard to all the circumstances, including the estimated amount of damages that individual class members may recover."[92]

The CAT's 2015 Guide to proceedings[93] amplifies these requirements. Without carrying out a full merits assessment, the CAT "will usually expect the strength of the claims to be more immediately perceptible in an opt-out than an opt-in case, since in the latter case, the class members have chosen to be part of the proceedings and may be presumed to have conducted their own assessment of the strength of their claim. (…) For example, where the claims seek damages for the consequence of an infringement which is covered by a decision of a competition authority (follow-on claims), they will generally be of sufficient strength for the purpose of this criterion." As to whether it is practicable for the proceedings to be brought in the opt-in scheme, the CAT "will consider all the circumstances, including the estimated amount of damages that individual class members may recover in determining whether it is practicable for the proceedings to be certified as opt-in." It has to be emphasized that "[t]here is a general preference for proceedings to be opt-in where practicable." "Indicators that an opt-in approach could be both workable and in the interests of justice might include the fact that the class is small but the loss suffered by each class member is high, or the fact that it is straightforward to identify and contact the class members."

In Slovenia, the law on collective actions was adopted in 2017 (and entered into force in April 2018).[94] It leaves the choice between the opt-in and the opt-out scheme to the court.[95] The opt-in system has to be used if non-pecuniary damages are involved or if at least 10% of group members has a claim in value exceeding EUR 2000. Nonetheless, even if the opt-out system is chosen by the court, group members not domiciled in Slovenia can become part of the proceedings only if they opt in.[96]

---

[90]Consumer Rights Act 2015. For a comprehensive analysis, see Rodger (2015).

[91]Section 47/B(7)(c) of the 1998 Competition Act. See Section 47/B(10)–(11).

[92]Section 79(3) of Competition Appeal Tribunal Rules 2015, Statutory Instrument 2015/1648.

[93]Section 6.39 of 2015 Competition Appeal Tribunal, Guide to proceedings. http://www.catribunal. org.uk/files/Guide_to_proceedings_2015.pdf. Accessed 20 April 2019.

[94]See Footnote 26.

[95]Article 29 of the Slovenian Law on Collective Actions. See British Institute of International and Comparative Law (2017: 14–15) and Sladič (2018: 214).

[96]Article 30 of the Slovenian Law on Collective Actions.

Seven Member States provide for the statutory right to opt-out collective litigation (in England this operates in addition to the foregoing competition law mechanism combining the opt-in and the opt-out system).[97]

Greece introduced opt-out collective actions very early, in 1994, in the field of consumer protection.[98] This vests certified consumer protection organizations with standing to claim damages on behalf of a group of injured consumers. Since its introduction, this mechanism has produced, on average, 2–3 cases per annum.[99]

The Portuguese collective action law dates back to 1995, long before this question became so topical in Europe, and has a constitutional basis.[100] The Portuguese provisions have a general application and enable actions for any civil claim, including financial relief. The general rules on popular actions (acção popular) are included in Act 83/95 and special provisions are to be found in particular fields, e.g. Law No. 19/2014 of 14 April on Environment Policy, Law No. 24/96 of 31 July on Consumer Protection, Law No. 107/2001 of 8 September on the Cultural Heritage, Securities Code and Law 23/2018 of 5 June on Antitrust Damages Actions. Notwithstanding the opt-out rule, the Portuguese popular action seems not to be particularly successful[101]; the information available suggests that the law's first decade saw only a few collective proceedings.[102]

The Spanish system[103] is a mixed opt-in-opt-out scheme with a restricted sectoral approach (it applies only to consumer matters).[104] In 2007, a similar provision was inserted as to matters concerning equal treatment between men and women.[105] Only some collective cases have made their way to court over the last thirty years, mostly injunctive actions. Collective actions are rare in practice due to their cost and the difficulty involved, first, in legally understanding what is needed to proceed with the action, and, second, in gathering group members and evidence and administering enforcement. In the recent years, an increase has been observed as a result of the economic downturn.[106] Notwithstanding the non-exhaustive and uncertain regulation

---

[97] As noted above, from these the United Kingdom also has, in the field of competition law, a scheme leaving the decision between the opt-in and opt-out scheme to the judge.

[98] See Footnote 23.

[99] Emvalomenos (2016: 6).

[100] Section 52(3) of the Portuguese Constitution.

[101] See Tortell (2008: 2–3, 5) and Rossi and Ferro (2013: 37–38).

[102] Tortell (2008: 10). Cf. Rossi and Ferro (2013: 65–66).

[103] Section 11 of Spanish Code on Civil Procedure (Ley 1/2000, de 7 de enero, de Enjuiciamiento Civil). For an English translation of the Spanish provisions, see de Cabiedes Hidalgo (2007a), for an analysis of the Spanish system, see de Cabiedes Hidalgo (2007b). Collective actions have been part of Spanish law since 1984. See Piñeiro (2016: 88).

[104] Gomez and Gili (2008: 6–7).

[105] Section 11bis introduced by L.O. 3/2007, de 22 de marzo, para la igualdad efectiva de mujeres y hombres («B.O.E.» 23 marzo).

[106] See Piñeiro (2015: 1055–1088).

of the field[107] and the absence of a settled practice,[108] 49 collective proceedings have been recorded until 2008.[109]

In Hungarian law, opt-out collective action mechanisms exist in competition law and consumer protection law, while an opt-in joint action scheme was introduced by the new Hungarian Code of Civil Procedure as to certain subject-matters (consumer protection, employment matters and environmental damages).[110] Although the opt-out mechanism has been in force for two decades, it has produced only a single published case where monetary relief was awarded.[111]

Bulgaria adopted an opt-out class action scheme in its Code of Civil Procedure of 2007.[112] However, courts continuously apply high requirements on class formation and representation, effectively transforming the procedure into an opt-in system, with the exception where the plaintiff is a public authority (the Commission on Consumer Protection) or a representative consumer association pursuing injunctive measures.[113] In terms of statutory language, the regime may cover all violations of law, though the case-law has the tendency to limit the scope to non-contractual violations.[114]

Besides consumer associations' usual power to request an injunction or a declaratory judgment on an opt-out basis,[115] the French Consumer Code (Code de la consommation) contains two patterns of collective action where monetary relief may be sought. First, in 1992 an opt-in scheme was inserted into the Consumer Code (action en représentation conjointe),[116] and subsequently introduced as to other matters (investor protection,[117] environmental protection). This appeared to be less efficient given that it produced, in the first one and a half decade of its history, only

---

[107]See Gomez and Gili (2008: 3). (No special procedure was introduced for collective proceedings and the respective rules are sometimes inconsistent, self-contradictory and gappy.)

[108]See Almoguera et al. (2004: 7).

[109]Gomez and Gili (2008: 51, 19–28).

[110]Sections 580-591 of the new Hungarian Code of Civil Procedure to go into effect on 1 January 2018 (Act CXXX of 2016 on the Code of Civil Procedure, in Hungarian: 2016. évi CXXX. törvény a polgári perrendtartásról). See Szalai (2017) and Udvary (2018).

[111]Case Gf.40336/2008/7 (Budapest High Court of Appeals), published under nr ÍH 2009.125.

[112]Promulgated in State Gazette No. 59/20.07.2007, amended and supplemented by SG No. 50/30.05.2008, modified by Judgment No. 3 of the Constitutional Court of the Republic of Bulgaria of 8.07.2008–SG No. 63/15.07.2008, amended by SG No. 69/5.08.2008. The class action provisions can be found in Chapter 33, Sections 379-388 of the Bulgarian Code of Civil Procedure.

[113]Markova (2015: 142–152).

[114]Katzarsky and Georgiev (2012: 64), para 1.2.

[115]Sections L621-1-L621-6 of the French Consumer Code (Code de la consommation). The French Commercial Code (Code de Commerce) also provides for the possibility of collective actions in respect of certain unfair competition mischiefs; the public prosecutor (ministère public), the minister of economic affairs and the head of the competition council have standing. Section L442-6 of the French Commercial Code. See Momège and Bessot (2004: 8).

[116]Loi n° 92-60, 18 janv. 1992 devenue les articles L. 422-1 à L. 422-3 du Code de la consommation, réd. Loi n° 93-949, 26 juillet 1993; R. 422-1 à 422-10, réd. Décr. n° 92-1306, 11 décembre 1992.

[117]L452-2 of the Monetary and Financial Code. See Magnier and Alleweldt (2008: 7–9).

a few cases.[118] Second, recently, in 2014, the French legislator inserted an opt-out collective action regime into the Consumer Code (action de groupe), which appears to be much more effective than the *ancien régime*, having produced seven cases in two years' time. This regime was extended to health care matters and, in 2016, converted into a general scheme applicable to discrimination, environmental protection, personal data[119] and health care matters.

English law provides for three options for collective litigation: two general procedural tools (representative proceedings, group litigation orders[120]) and a sectoral tool in competition law (where, as noted above, it is at the CAT's discretion to choose the opt-out scheme). Although representative proceedings may be carried out on an opt-out basis, they have remained ineffective due to the strict construction of the preconditions in the judicial practice.

5.2 Purview: Step-by-Step Evolution of a Precautious Revolution

Most European collective action laws have a limited (sectoral) purview[121] reflecting the notion that collective actions should be limited to cases where they are badly and obviously needed. Some Member States have used "leapfrogging" to extend the scheme to other sectors demonstrating the precautious approach of the European legal systems as to collective litigation.

In Greece, collective redress is available only in consumer protection law.[122] The Finnish Act on Collective Proceedings of 2007 applies exclusively to matters coming under the remit of the Consumer Ombudsman (consumer matters).[123] Italy introduced collective actions in the Consumer Code,[124] which may be used to pursue consumer claims arising from specific cases: standard contractual terms and conditions, defective products and services, unfair commercial practices and anti-

---

[118]See Magnier (2007: 14).

[119]Loi n° 2014-344 du 17 mars 2014 relative à la consommation et Décr. n° 2014-1081 du 24 sept. 2014 relatif à l'action de groupe en matière de consommation; Loi n° 2016-41 du 26 janv. 2016 de modernisation de notre système de santé et Décr. n° 2016-1249 du 26 sept. 2016 relatif à l'action de groupe en matière de santé; Loi n° 2016-1547 du 18 novembre 2016 de modernisation de la justice du XXIe siècle, JORF n° 0269 du 19 novembre 2016 texte n° 1.

[120]For an analysis of group litigation orders, see Mulheron (2014: 94–111).

[121]Commission Report on the implementation of the Commission Recommendation of 11 June 2013 on common principles for injunctive and compensatory collective redress mechanisms in the Member States concerning violations of rights granted under Union law (2013/396/EU), COM(2018) 40 final, p 3.

[122]Emvalomenos (2016: 2); British Institute of International and Comparative Law (2017: 181).

[123]See Footnote 51.

[124]Act 244 of 24 December 2007 and Act 99 of 23 July 2009. http://www.tedioli.com/Italian_class_action_text_english_version.pdf. Accessed 20 April 2019.

competitive conducts.[125] The purview of Maltese collective actions is confined to certain fields, such as competition, consumer protection and product safety law.[126] The Polish regime introduced in 2009[127] initially applied only to consumer law, product liability and tort liability (with the exception of the protection of personal interests) but was extended, in 2017, to claims resulting from the non-performance or undue performance of an obligation, unjust enrichment and certain infringements of personal interests (bodily injury or health disorder).[128] The Spanish class action rules[129] apply only to consumer matters.[130] In 2007, a similar provision was inserted as to matters concerning equal treatment between men and women.[131]

After the introduction of group actions in the field of consumer protection in 2014[132] and health care in January 2016,[133] in November 2016, the French legislator created a general framework for group actions.[134] The new regime extended the purview of the mechanism to discrimination, environmental protection, personal data and health care matters; consumer matters are not concerned by the general framework.[135]

Hungary introduced opt-out class actions in 1996 in the Competition Act and then in 1997 in the Consumer Protection Act.[136] Interestingly, while the operation of these systems attracted no criticism, the new Hungarian Code of Civil Procedure, having gone into effect on 1 January 2018, introduced an opt-in scheme applicable to consumer, employment and environmental tort matters.

---

[125] Section 140bis(2) of the Italian Consumer Code; Principe (2012). Recently, in *Adusbef v Monte dei Paschi di Siena*, the court of appeals of Florence held that retail investors are not consumers and, hence, are not covered by the Italian class action legislation. Afferni (2016: 85).

[126] See Footnote 69.

[127] Act on Class Actions of 17 December 2009 (Ustawa o dochodzeniu roszczeń w postępowaniu grupowym), published in Dziennik Ustaw), published in Journal of Laws of 2010, no 7; item. 44 p. 1.

[128] New Sections 1(2) and 1(2)(a)-(b) of the Polish Act on Class Actions.

[129] Section 11 of the Spanish Code of Civil Procedure.

[130] Gomez and Gili (2008: 6–7).

[131] Section 11bis of the Spanish Code of Civil Procedure.

[132] Loi n° 2014-344 du 17 mars 2014 relative à la consommation et Décr. n° 2014-1081 du 24 sept. 2014 relatif à l'action de groupe en matière de consommation.

[133] Loi n° 2016-41 du 26 janv. 2016 de modernisation de notre système de santé et Décr. n° 2016-1249 du 26 sept. 2016 relatif à l'action de groupe en matière de santé.

[134] Loi n° 2016-1547 du 18 novembre 2016 de modernisation de la justice du XXIe siècle, JORF n° 0269 du 19 novembre 2016 texte n° 1.

[135] Loi n° 2014-344 du 17 mars 2014 relative à la consommation et Décr. n° 2014-1081 du 24 sept. 2014 relatif à l'action de groupe en matière de consommation; Loi n° 2016-41 du 26 janv. 2016 de modernisation de notre système de santé et Décr. n° 2016-1249 du 26 sept. 2016 relatif à l'action de groupe en matière de santé; Loi n° 2016-1547 du 18 novembre 2016 de modernisation de la justice du XXIe siècle, JORF n° 0269 du 19 novembre 2016 texte n° 1.

[136] Act CLV of 1997 on consumer protection (1997. évi CLV. törvény a fogyasztóvédelemről).

The Slovenian regime on collective actions applies to consumer, competition, securities, labour and environmental law matters.[137]

The German model declaratory claim procedure introduced in 2018 applies solely to consumer matters.[138]

In English law, opt-out representative proceedings have been available long since, though they remained ineffective due to the strict construction of the preconditions in the judicial practice.[139] After introducing a general opt-in procedural tool (group litigation order),[140] the English government rejected the introduction of an opt-out scheme of general application and decided to introduce this mechanism on a sector-by-sector basis.[141] As a result, an opt-out scheme was made available in competition matters.[142]

The Belgian collective action was initially available only for consumers but in 2018 it was extended to SMEs.[143] It applies to cases where an enterprise[144] breaches one of its contractual obligations or violates one of the 31 (Belgian or European) laws enumerated in Section XVII.37 of the Code of Economic Law (Code de droit économique). These extend to fields like banking, competition law, consumer protection, energy, insurance, intellectual property, passengers' rights, payment and credit services, privacy, product safety and professional liability.[145]

A few Member States have collective action regimes of general application. The 2002 Swedish law on group proceedings, introducing an opt-in scheme effective as from 1 January 2003, covers the whole spectrum of civil claims (and not only specific sectors or branches of law).[146] Likewise, the Portuguese collective action law of 1995 has a general application and enables actions for any civil claim, including financial relief, albeit special provisions can be found also in particular fields, e.g. Law No. 19/2014 of 14 April on Environment Policy, Law No. 24/96 of 31 July on Consumer Protection, Law No. 107/2001 of 8 September on Cultural Heritage, Securities Code and Law 23/2018 of 5 June on Antitrust Damages Actions. The Bulgarian opt-out

---

[137] Article 2 of the Slovenian Law on Collective Actions. See Sladič (2018: 214); British Institute of International and Comparative Law (2017: 249). Article 2(2) refers to anti-discrimination disputes, however, it also provides that in this regard only collective injunctions are permissible.

[138] See Footnote 77.

[139] See Andrews (2001: 253).

[140] See Mulheron (2009: 427–431).

[141] The Government's Response to the Civil Justice Council's Report, Improving Access to Justice through Collective Actions (2009). See Hodges (2010: 376–379); Hodges (2009: 50–66).

[142] The Competition Appeal Tribunal specifies in the collective proceedings order whether the procedure has to be carried out in the opt-in or the opt-out system. Sections 47A-49E of Competition Act 1998, inserted by Part 1 of Schedule 8 of the Consumer Rights Act 2015.

[143] Loi portant modification, en ce qui concerne l'extension de l'action en réparation collective aux P.M.E., du Code de droit économique. 22 May 2018, Moniteur Belge (M.B.) (Official Gazette of Belgium, 22 May 2018). See Renier (2018).

[144] Section I.21 2° of the Belgian Code of Economic Law defines the group as a group of consumers or SMEs, while Sections XVII.36 and XVII.38 refer to a violation committed by an enterprise.

[145] Section XVII.37 of the Belgian Code of Economic Law.

[146] See Footnote 45.

collective action scheme inserted into the Code of Civil Procedure of 2007 also covers all violations of law, albeit the case-law has the tendency to limit the scope to injunctive measures concerning consumer disputes.[147] The Lithuanian system introduced in 2015 is also of general application.[148] The Danish rules on collective actions having gone into effect on 1 January 2008 introduced a generally applicable system where it is up to the judge to decide whether to approve the collective action under the opt-in or the opt-out scheme.

5.3 Pre-requisites of Collective Action and Certification

The pre-conditions of collective action in Europe normally extend to those of US class action (numerousity, commonality, typicality and adequate representation),[149] however, some systems go beyond this and require that the collective actions be expedient or superior to individual litigation and that the group be definable. The requirement of expediency contents itself with that the collective action is an appropriate means to enforce the claims of group members. Superiority goes beyond this expectation and requires that a collective action be more expedient than individual litigation. The latter has a higher significance in opt-out proceedings: these are expected to be more expedient than individual actions and definability plays a much more important role here, as group members are unknown, thus, the beneficiaries will have to be identified on the basis of the final judgment's group definition. Of course, legal counsels may go as far as possible with the common questions, to the extent permitted by the definability of the group, e.g. they may request the court to establish the legal basis (defendant's liability) but leave quantum to collective actions covering sub-classes or to individual litigation. In this sense, due to the requirements of superiority/expediency and definability, the purview of European collective actions is more restricted than that of their US counterpart.

It is worthy of note that some of the laws do not specify all the traditional requirements of collective action, such as numerousity, superiority and adequate representation. However, this may be due to the circumstance that owing to the rules on scope and standing, such a specification might appear to be redundant. Quite a few systems limit the availability of collective actions to consumer matters where it is assumed that a number of victims are concerned and they have small-claims which would be difficult to bring to court but for collective litigation. Similarly, several systems lean towards ensuring adequate representation through limiting standing to public entities and recognized civil organizations or through granting these plaintiffs a privileged status.

In France, opt-out collective actions may be launched if numerous persons (numerousity) placed in a similar situation suffer damages caused by the same person, the

---

[147] Katzarsky and Georgiev (2012: 64), para 1.2.
[148] Section 441[1] of the Lithuanian Code of Civil Procedure.
[149] See Udvary (2012: 37–40).

common cause of which is a similar breach of legal or contractual obligations (commonality).[150]

In Germany, model declaratory claims may be submitted only by qualified consumer protection organizations. It is noteworthy that heightened requirements apply here: in addition to the conditions applicable to organizations eligible to launch actions for an injunction, organizations engaging in actions for compensation need to fulfill extra requirements (adequate representation).[151] Furthermore, the matter is eligible if, at the time of submission, it is substantiated that it concerns at least 10 consumers and within two months after the procedure's publication at least 50 consumers register their cases (numerousity).[152]

Under Greek law, consumers' associations may bring consumer collective actions "for the protection of the general interests of the consuming public" or if "an illegal behavior hurts the interests of at least thirty (30) consumers."[153]

In Poland, the court certifies a collective action if the following conditions are met:

– numerousity (the group shall consist of at least 10 people)[154];
– commonality (the class action has to cover claims of the same kind and with the same or similar factual basis)[155];
– the Polish Act contains an idiosyncratic requirement which may be regarded as an emanation of the requirement of commonality: if a law-suit concerns a monetary claim, a collective action may be launched only if the amounts claimed by individual group members are equal; however, representative plaintiffs may obviate the problems emerging from this requirement through forming sub-classes and requesting a declaratory judgment.[156]

Section 140bis of the Italian Consumer Code establishes the following pre-conditions for collective actions:

– prima facie case (the claim is not manifestly unfounded);
– numerousity (a number of consumers is involved);
– homogeneity (the individual rights to be enforced are homogeneous);
– adequate representation (there is no conflict of interest between the group representative and group members and the group representative shall be capable of representing the group adequately).[157]

---

[150]"Lorsque plusieurs personnes placées dans une situation similaire subissent un dommage causé par une même personne, ayant pour cause commune un manquement de même nature à ses obligations légales ou contractuelles, une action de groupe peut être exercée en justice au vu des cas individuels présentés par le demandeur." Section 62 of Loi n° 2016-1547 du 18 novembre 2016 de modernisation de la justice du XXIe siècle.

[151]Section 606(3)1 of the German Code of Civil Procedure.

[152]Section 606(3)2-3 of the German Code of Civil Procedure.

[153]Articles 10(16) of Law 2251/1994 on Consumers' Protection.

[154]Section 1(1) of the Polish Act on Pursuing Claims in Group Proceedings.

[155]See Footnote 154.

[156]Sections 2(1) and 2(2) of the Polish Act on Pursuing Claims in Group Proceedings.

[157]Section 140-bis(6) of the Italian Consumer Code.

In Malta, the court certifies[158] "the proceedings as appropriate for collective proceedings" if they "raise common issues" (commonality)[159] and "are the most appropriate means for the fair and efficient resolution of the common issues" (superiority).[160] Interestingly, the law expressly excludes the requirement of numerousity when it provides that "the proceedings are brought on behalf of an identified class of two or more persons." The law sets out requirements as to the adequacy of group representation: a registered consumers' association (or ad hoc constituted body) or a group member may be approved, if the court "is satisfied that the class representative (a) would fairly and adequately act in the interests of the class members; and (b) does not have, in relation to the common issues for the class members, a material interest that is in conflict with the interests of the class members."[161]

A collective action may be launched in Bulgaria, if the following requirements are met:

– commonality (a collective action may be certified if group members' common interests were impaired by the same infringement and this may give rise to similar legal consequences for all of them)[162];
– definability (group members are identifiable)[163];
– adequate representation (it has to be proved that the group representative has the capacity "to protect the harmed interest seriously and in good faith, as well as to incur the charges related to the conduct of the case, including the costs").[164]

The requirement of numerousity does not appear in the Bulgarian Code on Civil Procedure.[165]

In Sweden, the institution of group proceedings is subject to the following preconditions.

---

[158] Article 9(1) of the Maltese Collective Proceedings Act.

[159] Article 2 of the Maltese Collective Proceedings Act defines the term "common issues" as follows: "(i) common but not necessarily identical issues of fact, or (ii) common but not necessarily identical issues of law that arise from common but not necessarily identical facts." Article 10 provides that "[t]he court shall not refuse to decree proceedings as collective proceedings solely on any of the following grounds: (a) the claim requires individual assessment after determination of the common issues; (b) the claim relates to separate contracts involving different class members; (c) the amount and nature of the damages sought vary among the different class members."

[160] As to superiority, among others, the following circumstances need to be taken into account: "(a) the benefits of the proposed collective proceedings; and (b) the nature of the class." Article 9(2) of the Maltese Collective Proceedings Act.

[161] Article 12 of the Maltese Collective Proceedings Act.

[162] Katzarsky and Georgiev (2012: 64–65), para 1.6.

[163] Section 379(1) of the Bulgarian Code of Civil Procedure.

[164] Sections 380(3) and 381(1) of the Bulgarian Code of Civil Procedure. The requirement of financial ability played a central role in a case where the class action initiated by a consumer association against a leasing company was dismissed when the court established that the plaintiff held a little more than BGN 3400 (approximately € 1700) in its bank account. This was deemed insufficient in the case, which concerned over 30,000 lease contracts. Ruling no 5951 of 14 November 2016 on case no. 7904/2013 of Sofia City Court, Commercial Division, panel VI-9.

[165] See Section 379 of the Bulgarian Code of Civil Procedure; Katzarsky and Georgiev (2012: 64), para 1.5.

– commonality ("the action is founded on circumstances that are common or of a similar nature for the claims of the members of the group");
– expediency ("group proceedings do not appear to be inappropriate owing to some claims of the members of the group, as regards grounds, differing substantially from other claims");
– superiority ("the larger part of the claims to which the action relates cannot equally well be pursued by personal actions by the members of the group");
– definability ("the group, taking into consideration its size, ambit and otherwise, is appropriately defined");
– adequate representation ("the plaintiff, taking into consideration the plaintiff's interest in the substantive matter, the plaintiff's financial capacity to bring a group action and the circumstances generally, is appropriate to represent the members of the group in the case").[166]

In Finland, collective proceedings may be launched in consumer matters, if the following requirements are met:

– numerousity ("several persons have claims");
– commonality ("several persons have claims against the same defendant, based on the same or similar circumstances");
– expediency ("the hearing of the case as a class action is expedient in view of the size of the class, the subject-matter of the claims presented in it and the proof offered in it");
– definability ("the class has been defined with adequate precision").[167]

In Denmark, a collective action may be initiated, if the following substantive conditions are met:

– commonality (the parties dispose of a common claim arising from the same factual and legal basis);
– superiority (the collective action is the best mechanism to settle the claims; this condition is met, if the collective action is more expedient than traditional joinder of parties);
– definability (group members are identifiable and may be informed in an appropriate manner);
– technicality (the judge disposes of the expertise required to adjudicate the claims);
– adequate representation (an appropriate person can be appointed as the group's representative).[168]

---

[166] Section 8 of the Swedish Group Proceedings Act.
[167] Section 2 of the Finnish Act on Class Action.
[168] Møgelvang-Hansen (2008: 4).

In Hungary, the pre-conditions of collective action under the Competition Act and the Consumer Protection Act may be boiled down to the following requirements[169]:

- numerousity (the violation concerns numerous consumers);
- definability (the victims of the violation are identifiable on the basis of the circumstances of the violation);
- adequate representation is not expressly required, however, as standing is conferred solely on public bodies and recognized consumer rights organizations (on the Hungarian Competition Office as to the Competition Act and on the consumer protection agency, the public prosecutor and consumer rights organizations as to the Consumer Protection Act), such a specification seems to be redundant.

Under the new Hungarian Code of Civil Procedure, the court certifies an opt-in collective action, if the following conditions are met[170]:

- numerousity (the joint action may be certified, if at least 10 plaintiffs join)[171];
- commonality—identity (the plaintiffs may bring to court one or more rights that are, in terms of content, identical in relation to all plaintiffs—"representative right"—, if the facts sustaining the representative right are, in essence, the same in relation to all plaintiffs (representative facts) and it can be proved that the individual plaintiffs are entitled to the representative right—"linking")[172];
- superiority (the court may decline the request for certification, if it is not reasonable to certify the collective action given that the burden in terms of work and time related to the action's collective nature would be so huge that the collective proceedings' efficiency benefits would likely vanish).[173]

In Lithuania, the Code of Civil Procedure establishes the following preconditions for collective actions[174]:

- numerousity ("an action shall be lodged by at least 20 natural and/or legal entities that express their will to be members of the class and bring the action to the court in writing"),[175]
- commonality (the action has to be "grounded on identical or similar factual circumstances" and to aim at "protecting natural or legal entities that set up a class and brought a claim, identical or similar substantive rights or interests protected by the law by means of the same remedy"),[176]

---

[169]Section 92(1) of the Hungarian Competition Act; Section 39(1) of the Hungarian Consumer Protection Act.

[170]Section 585(1)-(2) of the new Hungarian Code of Civil Procedure.

[171]Sections 583(1) and 585(1)(a) of the new Hungarian Code of Civil Procedure.

[172]Sections 583(1) and 585(1)(b)-(e) of the new Hungarian Code of Civil Procedure.

[173]Section 585(1)(f) of the new Hungarian Code of Civil Procedure. The Code's explanatory memorandum confirms that this is a superiority requirement, as the court has to investigate whether the joint action is more efficient than pursuing the claims individually.

[174]Section 441^3 of the Lithuanian Code of Civil Procedure.

[175]Section 441^3(2)(1) of the Lithuanian Code of Civil Procedure.

[176]Sections 441^1(2) and 441^3(1)(1) of the Lithuanian Code of Civil Procedure.

- superiority (the "class action is a more expedient, effective and appropriate means of resolving the particular dispute than individual actions"),[177]
- adequate representation ("the class shall be represented by an appropriate representative"[178] and "by an attorney-at-law"[179]).[180]

Spanish law does not specify the pre-conditions of collection actions in consumer matters, though, it attaches high importance to definability.[181]

Although representative proceedings are available under English law if more than one person has the same interest in a claim, they have been rarely used due to the strict judicial interpretation of the pre-conditions. While definability is not specified by the law, courts have been reluctant to endorse representative proceedings where group members were not readily ascertainable. In *Emerald Supplies Ltd and Others v British Airways plc*[182] flower importers sued British Airways, because it participated in an anti-competitive collusion resulting in the increase of carriage fees. Emerald, who represented the plaintiffs, sued both on behalf of direct and indirect purchasers, and the court came to the conclusion that the procedure was not representative as at the moment when it was instituted group members could not be determined and did not have a common interest.

If the damages suffered by the group and the loss sustained by individual group members are not ascertainable, claims for damages may be pursued in a two-stage procedure. Accordingly, in the first phase, a declaratory judgment is requested in respect of the issues the group members have in common. Thereafter, individual group members may institute separate actions for damages, where they may rely on the judicial determination of the common issues.[183]

In competition law, the Competition Appeal Tribunal (CAT) may certify[184] a collective action (collective proceedings order, CPO), if the claims arise from a competition law violation,[185] they "raise the same, similar or related issues of fact or law" (commonality), "are brought on behalf of an identifiable class of persons"

---

[177]Section 441³(1)(2) of the Lithuanian Code of Civil Procedure.

[178]Section 441³(1)(4) of the Lithuanian Code of Civil Procedure.

[179]Section 441³(2)(2) of the Lithuanian Code of Civil Procedure. See also Section 441¹(3) of the Lithuanian Code of Civil Procedure.

[180]In addition to the above-listed substantive pre-conditions, Lithuanian law also erects a procedural (pre-trial dispute settlement) requirement: the defendant has to be notified of the intention to file a class action and has to be given at least 30 days to meet the group's demands. See Sections 441³(1)3) and 441² of the Lithuanian Code of Civil Procedure.

[181]Gomez and Gili (2008: 6).

[182][2009] EWHC 741 (Ch).

[183]*Prudential Assurance Co. V. Newman Indus. Ltd.*, 2 W.L.R. 339 (Ch 1980).

[184]For an analysis of the CAT's decision practice, see Veljanovski (2019).

[185]Section 47/A(2) of the 1998 Competition Act

(definability),[186] "are suitable to be brought in collective proceedings" (expediency)[187] and adequate representation is secured.[188]

The certification of the first two collective actions was dismissed by the CAT.[189] However, in one of these, in *Merricks v Mastercard Incorporated & Anor*,[190] the case was remanded by the Court of Appeal, which held that the certification of a claim and the grant of a collective proceedings order (CPO) may not be refused merely because individual losses cannot be ascertained. The CAT refused certification because of "the absence of any plausible means of calculating the loss of individual claimants so as to devise an appropriate method of distributing any aggregate award of damages."[191] The Court of Appeal overturned the CAT's decision, ruling that

> The CAT is expressly required under Rule 79(2) to take into account whether the claims are suitable for an aggregate award of damages when considering whether to make a CPO but not whether such an award can be distributed in any particular manner. The making of an aggregate award does not (...) require the Court to calculate individual loss or importantly to assess the damages included in that award on an individual basis. Why, then, should they be distributed in that way?[192]

> More importantly, for present purposes, the CAT is not required under Rule 79(2)(f) for certification purposes to consider more than whether the claims are suitable for an aggregate award of damages which, by definition, does not include the assessment of individual loss. Distribution is a matter for the trial judge to consider following the making of an aggregate award: see Rules 92 and 93. We therefore consider that it was both premature and wrong for the CAT to have refused certification by reference to the proposed method of distribution: an error compounded by their view that distribution must be capable of being carried out by some means which corresponds to individual loss.[193]

Interestingly, the collective proceedings order is not conditioned on numerosity: a collective action may be certified, if it combines "two or more claims."[194] Furthermore, though the statutory language does not go beyond the requirement of suitability, the Competition Appeal Tribunal Rules of 2015 contain a list of factors to be taken into account as to the interpretation of the requirement of suitability and these suggest that collective proceedings may be certified only if they are more efficient than individual actions (superiority). Notably, the CAT takes into account not only whether the collective action is "an appropriate means for the fair and efficient resolution of the common issues" but also its costs and benefits, whether individual actions have already been commenced and the size and nature of the group.[195]

---

[186] Section 79(1)(a) of Competition Appeal Tribunal Rules 2015, Statutory Instrument 2015/1648.

[187] Section 47/B(6) of the 1998 Competition Act.

[188] Section 47/B(5) of the 1998 Competition Act.

[189] *Gibson v Pride* [2017] CAT 9; *Merricks v Mastercard* [2017] CAT 16. See Veljanovski (2019).

[190] [2019] EWCA Civ 674 (16 April 2019).

[191] Para 29.

[192] Para 60.

[193] Para 62.

[194] Section 47/B(1) of the 1998 Competition Act.

[195] Section 79(2) of Competition Appeal Tribunal Rules 2015, Statutory Instrument 2015/1648.

Any person may be appointed as group representative, if he is capable of representing the group adequately. The representative does not need to be a class member, the CAT may appoint any person if it "considers that it is just and reasonable for that person to act as a representative in those proceedings."[196] Concerning the adequacy of the representative, the CAT will take into account, among others, whether there is a conflict of interest, the representative's ability to cover the defendant's legal costs if ordered to do so,[197] whether the representative has a plan concerning the litigation strategy, the notification of group members, governance issues and estimated costs.[198]

In Belgium, the law erects two requirements: superiority and adequate representation. A collective action may be certified only if it is more effective than individual litigation[199] and the judge considers representation to be adequate.[200] Interestingly, as noted above, although standing is reserved for authorized non-profit organizations, adequacy of representation has to be inquired separately. As regards the superiority of collective litigation, the court may consider the following factors: size of the group, the relationship between individual damages and collective harm and the collective action's complexity and efficiency.[201]

5.4 Standing and Adequate Representation

According to the general opinion, contrary to the US pattern, in the European Union standing is reserved for public entities (administrative agencies, the attorney general etc.) and qualified non-profit civil organizations such as consumer protection NGOs. According to European thinking, conferring standing on these public and not-for-profit organizations with the exclusion of group members and for-profit entities mitigates the risk of abuse. It is argued that because these organizations are not profit-orientated, they are attentive to the public interest, furthermore, they are registered, regulated and supervised. However, in fact, while the heroes of class actions are certainly not group members (representative parties) but public entities and civil organizations, in quite a few Member States, their standing operates in parallel to that of group members and only a few European legal systems limit standing exclusively to public entities and non-profit organizations. Nonetheless, there is a clear tendency to reserve "hard cases" (which are difficult to manage or raise higher risks of abuse) to public entities and recognized civil organizations. Such cases involve opt-out proceedings and cases where it is difficult to define the group.

---

[196] Sections 47/B(2) and 47/B(8) of the 1998 Competition Act.

[197] Section 78(3) of Competition Appeal Tribunal Rules 2015, Statutory Instrument 2015/1648.

[198] Section 78(3) of the 2015 Competition Appeal Tribunal Rules, Statutory Instrument 2015/1648.

[199] Section XVII.36 3° of the Belgian Code of Economic Law.

[200] Section XVII.36 2° of the Belgian Code of Economic Law.

[201] Voet (2016: 2).

In Finland, solely the Consumer Ombudsman has the power to institute a collective action.[202] In France, only recognized civil associations whose object extends to the protection of the interests at stake may institute opt-out proceedings.[203] In Belgium, only authorized consumer associations, SMEs' organizations and non-profit organizations may launch collective actions. However, the law distinguishes between standing and adequacy of representation: the latter has to be examined independently. Interestingly, the Consumer Mediation Service (Service de médiation pour le consommateur") may also launch collective proceedings but only for negotiating a collective settlement; if no settlement can be achieved, a consumer association has to step in to continue the procedure.[204] In Germany, model declaratory claims may be submitted solely by qualified consumer protection organizations that—in addition to the conditions applicable to entities eligible to launch actions for injunction—meet five extra conditions: they have a membership made up of at least 10 associations or 350 natural persons, have been registered for four years as authorized to launch consumer actions for injunction, are engaged in non-professional educational or advisory activities, do not submit the model declaratory claim for for-profit considerations and do not gather more than 5% of their financial resources through company donations.[205] The law suggests that in case of actions for compensation, the group representative needs to meet heightened requirements as compared to actions for an injunction. It is noteworthy that, legally speaking, no compensation is awarded in the German procedure, the court may merely establish that the pre-conditions of the defendant's liability are met. In the same vein, in Greece, standing is conferred exclusively on certified consumer protection associations ("consumer unions") that have at least 500 active members (if more than one association files the case, they need to have 500 active members jointly) and have been registered for at least one year.[206] In Slovenia, standing is conferred on representative non-profit organizations and the attorney general.[207]

In Lithuania, collective action may be launched by a group member, an association or a trade union "where the pleas laid in the class claim arise out of legal relations directly related to the objective and field of activity of the association or the trade union and where at least 10 members of the class are the members of the association or trade union. Members of the class may include not only the members of the association or the trade union and in the lawsuit proceedings the association or the trade union shall represent the interests of all members of the class."[208]

---

[202] See Footnote 51.

[203] Section 63 of Loi n° 2016-1547 du 18 novembre 2016 de modernisation de la justice du XXIe siècle.

[204] Section XVII.39 of the Belgian Code of Economic Law.

[205] Section 606(1)2 of the German Code of Civil Procedure.

[206] Articles 10(16)-(17) of Law 2251/1994 on Consumers' Protection.

[207] Article 4 of the Slovenian Law on Collective Actions.

[208] Section 441^4(1)-(2) of the Lithuanian Code of Civil Procedure.

In Hungary, the Competition Act confers standing on the Hungarian Competition Office and the Consumer Protection Act on public entities (consumer protection agency, public prosecutor) and consumer rights organizations. In opt-in procedures launched under the new Code of Civil Procedure, standing is conferred on group members, who, before submitting the claim, have to conclude a joint action contract which, among others, has to name the group representative.

Polish law confers standing on class members and the regional consumer ombudsman (a public body).[209]

In Malta, both registered consumers' associations (and ad hoc constituted bodies) and group members may be approved as group representative. The law establishes requirements to ensure adequate representation: the court approves the group representative if it is satisfied that he "(a) would fairly and adequately act in the interests of the class members; and (b) does not have, in relation to the common issues for the class members, a material interest that is in conflict with the interests of the class members."[210]

In Sweden, collective proceedings may be initiated by group members (private group action), civil organizations (NGO action) and administrative agencies (public group action).[211]

Portuguese law also defines standing widely: citizens, associations, foundations and municipalities (for the protection of the citizens living in their territory) may institute an action.[212]

In Bulgaria, standing is conferred on group members and civil organizations.[213]

In Spain, standing is conferred on group members, consumer organizations and public entities. The Spanish Code of Civil Procedure distinguishes between general interests (intereses generales) and collective interests (interses colectivos). The former concern an undetermined number of consumers and can be protected in an injunctive class action. Public entities (such as the Public Ministry and entities named in special consumer legislation) and representative consumer organizations have standing to bring them before courts.[214] Collective interests are those where consumers are already identified or can be easily identified; these can be brought before courts by group members, representative consumer associations and public entities (such as the Public Ministry and entities named by special consumer legislation). In this

---

[209] Section 4(2) of the Polish Act on Pursuing Claims in Group Proceedings.

[210] Article 12 of the Maltese Collective Proceedings Act. See British Institute of International and Comparative Law (2017: 217).

[211] Sections 2(3) and 3-6 of the Swedish Group Proceedings Act. See Pettersson et al. (2004: 4).

[212] Article 19 of Law 23/2018 of 5 June on Antitrust Damages Actions also grants standing to business associations.

[213] Section 379(2)-(3) of the Bulgarian Code on Civil Procedure.

[214] Section 11(5) of the Spanish Code of Civil Procedure, conferring standing on the Spanish Public Prosecutor (Ministerio Fiscal), was inserted in 2014. Ley 3/2014, de 27 de marzo, por la que se modifica el texto refundido de la Ley General para la Defensa de los Consumidores y Usuarios y otras leyes complementarias, aprobado por el R.D. Legislativo 1/2007, de 16 de noviembre («B.O.E.» 28 marzo). See de Ávila Ruiz-Peinado (2016: 14).

case, a group action is launched. Special consumer legislation may also provide for the possibility to accumulate both types of actions.[215]

In Denmark, the group representative is appointed by the court, who may be a group member, an association, a private institute or other organization or an administrative agency (e.g. the Consumer Ombudsman). As noted above, under Danish law, the court has the discretion to decide whether the case should be tried in the opt-in or the opt-out scheme. If the action follows the opt-out pattern, only an administrative agency may be appointed as group representative.

The Italian collective action may be initiated by any consumer. Albeit that the consumer may also authorize a consumer organization,[216] standing goes to the consumer who initiated the procedure.

In England, group litigation order and representative actions may be launched by group members, while (in the United Kingdom) competition law collective actions may be launched by a group member or a representative body.

5.5   Status of Group Members in Opt-in Proceedings: Liability for Legal Costs and Res Judicata Effect

Although opt-in collective litigation is based on group members' explicit approval, in most systems members are, at least formally, not parties to the procedure and this quality is conferred on the group representative. As a corollary, group members are normally affected by the outcome of the case (that is, are covered by the judgment's res judicata effects) but they are usually not liable for the prevailing defendant's legal costs. This is a risk that is normally borne by the group representative. The rationale of this approach is more practical than doctrinal. As group members expressly join the group, it would be plausible, both doctrinally and constitutionally, to expect them to run the risks attached to failure. Nonetheless, as a matter of practice, it would be rather difficult to have them join in matters where the claim is small. The information asymmetry between the members and the group representative may warrant that this risk be placed on the latter.

Under Swedish law, the cost-shifting burdens those who launched the action (group representative) and not group members, who are not considered to be parties to the proceedings. Accordingly, if the litigation is successful, group members receive their net claim; if the litigation is unsuccessful, the defendant's legal costs are shifted on the group representative.[217] Likewise, in Finland, the traditional "loser

---

[215]Royal Legislative Decree 1/2007 consolidating the 1984 Law on Consumer Protection and other consumer laws have reduced the number of these laws, of which there were over twenty-five. Some still remained, and include rules on collective actions, such as Sections 32 and 33 of Law 3/1991 of 10 January on Unfair Competition, and Section 6 of Law 34/1988 of 11 November on Advertising. See Piñeiro (2016: 90–91).

[216]Section 140bis(1) of the Italian Consumer Code.

[217]Sections 33-36 and 41 of the Swedish Group Proceedings Act.

pays" principle applies also to group proceedings but group members are not parties to the proceedings, hence, if joining the action, they do not run any risk in terms of legal costs.[218] Italian law's two-way cost-shifting rule is maintained also as to collective actions. However, in case the court decides against the plaintiff, it orders the group representative (and not group members) to reimburse the defendant for his reasonable legal costs. In Germany law, the model declaratory claim is submitted by the organization representing the group, which qualifies as a party and runs the risks related to legal costs.[219]

The mixed regime available in Slovenia maintains the two-way cost shifting rule,[220] nonetheless, group members are, formally, not parties to the collective action[221] and have no right to claim reimbursement and are not responsible for reimbursing the defendant.[222]

Nonetheless, a couple of opt-in systems do stick to the full application of the "loser pays" principle, insisting on the notion that if someone wants to have a chance for a favorable award, he also has to carry the risk of being liable for the expenses the action generates.

In Malta, although the "costs may be awarded in favour or against the class representative, but may not be awarded in favour of or against a represented person who is not the class representative",[223] the collective proceedings agreement, which is an agreement between the group members and the group representative and which is accepted by group members when joining the proceedings, "may also include provision for the pre-payment and, or reimbursement of any judicial costs incurred by the class representative, [p]rovided that every class member shall only be liable for costs in proportion to his claim."[224]

Danish law did not discard group members' liability for legal costs in opt-in proceedings. The court may provide that the group representative and joining group members have to bestow a security for legal costs; if the court decides so, no additional financial contribution may be requested from group members; that is, this sum functions as a cap on individual group members' liability for legal costs.[225]

Likewise, group members (and not the group representative) are liable for the legal costs in the opt-in scheme established by the Hungarian Code of Civil Procedure. Before launching the action, group members have to conclude a "joint action contract", which lists, among others, the plaintiffs, names the representative plaintiff

---

[218] Viitanen (2008: 8).

[219] See Entwurf eines Gesetzes zur Einführung einer zivilprozessualen Musterfeststellungsklage. https://www.bmjv.de/SharedDocs/Gesetzgebungsverfahren/Dokumente/RegE_Musterfeststellungsklage.pdf?__blob=publicationFile&v=2.15 and 26. Accessed on 20 March 2019.

[220] Article 60 of the Slovenian Law on Collective Actions; Sladič (2018: 215).

[221] Zdolšek et al. (2018: 231).

[222] "[U]nless the costs are caused by the group members' fault." Article 62 of the Slovenian Law on Collective Actions.

[223] Article 23(1) of the Maltese Collective Proceedings Act.

[224] Article 2 of the Maltese Collective Proceedings Act.

[225] Møgelvang-Hansen (2008: 7–8).

and its deputy and contains provisions on the advancement, bearing and split of costs, the preparation of the action and legal costs, the responsibility of the representative plaintiff, including its liability for damages.[226] The "joint action contract" also has to determine the conditions of adhesion and withdrawal,[227] it has to contain provisions on settlement, that is, whether a settlement may be concluded or not, and if it may, it also has to establish the minimum amount and other related conditions,[228] it has to make provision for whether the representative plaintiff's declarations have to be approved by the parties (group members).[229] Sections 586(1)(l) and 586(2) of the Hungarian Code of Civil Procedure expressly provide that the parties' share from the money awarded by the court or provided for in the settlement has to be commensurate to the proportion represented by the value of the individual party's claim and the parties may not agree otherwise. As it is banned to agree to a division that departs from the proportions of the values of the claims, the parties may not enter into arrangements where some members take higher risks in exchange for a higher share in the money awarded. Hungarian law follows the "loser pays" principle and, at the end of the day, group members run the risk of being responsible for the successful defendant's legal costs. Although legal costs are awarded to and against the representative plaintiff,[230] as noted above, in the joint action contract, group members have to reach an agreement as to the advancement, bearing and split of these costs.

In European opt-in systems, the res judicata effects extend to those group members who expressly join the group. In Sweden, the judgment covers those group members who expressly join the group and, accordingly, the judgment covers the claims of these persons (res judicata effect).[231] Similarly, settlements, which are to be approved by the court, bind only those who join the group.[232] In Finland, the group consists of those persons who get their declarations of accession to the Ombudsman within the deadline established by the court.[233] The judgment's legal effects cover solely those group members who opted in.[234] In Malta, the collective judgment on the common issues binds only those group members who joined the proceedings.[235] In Germany, courts have no power to award damages, instead, the purpose of the action is to establish that the claim's or legal relationship's factual and legal pre-conditions exist or do not exist.[236] Group members may seek monetary relief, on an individual basis, after the pre-conditions of the defendant's liability are established. The final declaratory judgment is binding on courts in matters between consumers who opted

---

[226] Sections 586(1)(a)-(c), 586(1)(e) & 586(1)(g) of the Hungarian Code of Civil Procedure.

[227] Section 586(1)(h) of the Hungarian Code of Civil Procedure.

[228] Section 586(1)(i) of the Hungarian Code of Civil Procedure.

[229] Section 586(1)(j) of the Hungarian Code of Civil Procedure.

[230] Section 590(3) of the Hungarian Code of Civil Procedure.

[231] Sections 13-14 of the Swedish Group Proceedings Act.

[232] Section 26 of the Swedish Group Proceedings Act.

[233] See Footnote 50.

[234] Viitanen (2008: 5).

[235] Article 18(1) of the Maltese Collective Proceedings Act.

[236] See Footnote 77.

in and the defendant, provided these concern the same aims and the same fact pattern as the collective declaratory judgment.[237] In Italy, the final judgment is binding on all group members who joined the proceedings (and the lead plaintiff and the defendant obviously). While those who failed to join are not bound, the class action has a preclusion effect as to future collective actions in the same subject: consumers not part of the group do retain their rights to launch individual law-suits but may not start another collective action against the same defendant on identical grounds.[238] In UK competition law's opt-in scheme, if the CAT carries out the procedure according to the opt-in principle, the CAT's judgments and orders will be binding only on those group members who opted in.[239] In Lithuania, final court decisions are binding on group members who opted in. The court may adjudicate the pleas common to all class members in a "common ruling"; in case class members have individual pleas, the court may adopt an "intermediate ruling" and "individual rulings."[240]

5.6 Status of Group Members in Opt-Out Proceedings: Liability for Legal Costs, Res Judicata Effect and the "Only Benefits" Principle

As noted above, due to doctrinal and constitutional reasons, European opt-out collective actions have been impregnated by the "only benefits" principle: the encroachment on party autonomy may be justified if only benefits accrue to group members. European systems have been struggling remarkably with the implementation of this principle, producing innovative and idiosyncratic solutions.

The major risks related to collective litigation in Europe are the liability for legal costs and being bound by an unfavorable judgment in case the group representative fails.

Due to the two-way cost-shifting rule, the prevailing party has to be compensated for his reasonable legal costs. It is evident that in opt-out proceedings group members may not be liable for any legal costs (except the ones they caused). Likewise, the possibility of introducing the American rule as to collective actions was also generally rejected—it would have been inconsistent to do away with an entrenched principle of European civil procedure as to collective litigation, while preserving it as to individual actions. These two factors determined that it should be the group representative who carries the risk of legal costs.

In the Greek consumer collective action, group members are not liable for legal costs if the collective action proves unsuccessful.[241] Likewise, in Portugal, it is the

---

[237] See Footnote 78.

[238] Afferni (2016: 89–90).

[239] Sections 47B(12) and 59(1) of the 1998 Competition Act.

[240] Section 441^9 and Section 261^1 of the Lithuanian Code of Civil Procedure.

[241] European Parliament, Policy Department A: Economic and Scientific Policy, Directorate General for Internal Policies (2011: 25).

group representative (collective plaintiff) and not individual group members who carries the risk as to legal costs.[242] The same approach prevails in Spain. In order to promote collective actions, Article 37(d) of Royal Legislative Decree 1/2007 laid down the right of consumer associations' to legal aid. In Hungary, in opt-out proceedings, group members are not liable for legal costs, contrary to the opt-in scheme of the Hungarian Code of Civil Procedure. In the United Kingdom's opt-out scheme available (subject to the CAT's discretion) in competition matters, the risks related to legal costs are, in principle, run by the group representative: "costs may be awarded to or against the class representative, but may not be awarded to or against a represented person who is not the class representative."[243] In Bulgaria, group members are not liable for legal costs if the collective action proves unsuccessful—the main burden is assumed by the group representative, who is required to prove his financial capacity at the outset of the procedure.[244] However, group members who expressly opted in would be also liable together with the group representative. Once they opt in, they become parties to the proceedings with the pertinent rights that allow them to influence the course of the case, which, in turn, allows the imposition of liability in case of failure.

Danish law subjects group members to partial liability for legal costs, while trying to preserve the "only benefits" principle: if the proceedings are conducted in the opt-out pattern, group members cannot be obliged to pay more for legal costs than the money actually awarded to them.[245] In other words, group members run the risk of losing money with the group action only if the opt-in scheme is used and they join the action.[246]

Legal costs are not the only risk where the need of the "only benefits" principle has been claimed. While most European opt-out systems simply extend the judgment's res judicata effects to group members who did not opt-out, a few Member States were influenced by the argument that party autonomy is restricted also if individual group members could have achieved a better result than the one the group representative did (they could have won in a case where the collective action failed or could have obtained a more favorable remedy). As it is virtually impossible to assess this on a case-by-case basis, some European systems (Hungary, Portugal, France) have developed various practices to ensure the judgment's res judicata effect without formally extending it to group members and made the judgment's binding force limping.

The majority of European opt-out regimes uses a straight approach and provides that the judgment's res judicata effect covers all group members but those who opted out.

---

[242]Tortell (2008: 7).

[243]Section 98 of Competition Appeal Tribunal Rules 2015, Statutory Instrument 2015/1648.

[244]Section 380 (3) in conjunction with Section 381 (3) of the Bulgarian Code on Civil Procedure.

[245]See Footnote 225.

[246]Nielsen and Linhart (2012: 238).

In Bulgaria, group members may opt-in but the judgment will extend to all group members who did not opt-out.

> The judgment of the court shall have effect in respect of the infringer, the person or persons who have brought the action, as well as in respect of those persons who claim that they are harmed by the established infringement and who have not declared that they wish to pursue a remedy independently in a separate procedure. The excluded persons may avail themselves of the judgment whereby the class action has been granted.[247]

In Spain, group members may participate in the procedure.[248] Once the court confirms the collective action, this fact has to be announced.[249] The court's judgment has to give a detailed definition of the features and requirements that are to be met to qualify as a group member. The judgment rendered as a result of a collective action and its res judicata effects cover all group members, eventually also those, who did not opt in. If the court decides for the plaintiffs, the judgment has to determine the consumers and users benefiting from the judgment individually. When group members cannot be identified, the judgment has to set out the conditions of group membership and establish the data, characteristics and requirements that are to be met for claiming payment or requesting enforcement.[250] If consumers are not determined individually in the judgment, a writ has to be issued in the enforcement stage to establish whether a particular person, on the basis of the data, characteristics and requirements set out there, is covered by the judgment.[251]

In Denmark, as noted above, the court has the power to decide whether to carry out the proceedings in the opt-in or the opt-out scheme. The parties of the procedure are the group representative and the adversary party (defendant); group members are not parties in the conventional sense.[252] Nevertheless, in the opt-out procedure, the judgment's res judicata effects extend to the members who failed to opt out.

A similar scheme prevails in Belgium: the court has the power to decide between the opt-in and the opt-out scheme. The final judgment extends, accordingly, to those who opted in or opted out, depending on the scheme chosen by the court.[253]

In the United Kingdom, in competition matters, it is up to the CAT to decide whether the procedure will be carried out in the opt-in or the opt-out scheme.[254] In case the opt-out system is used, the CAT's judgments and orders will be binding on those who did not opt out.[255] Class members domiciled outside the UK, to be covered by the CAT's judgments or orders, have to opt in, even if the opt-out scheme

---

[247]Section 386(1) of the Bulgarian Code on Civil Procedure.

[248]Section 13(1) of the Spanish Code of Civil Procedure.

[249]Section 15 of the Spanish Code of Civil Procedure.

[250]Sections 221 and 222(3) of Spanish Code of Civil Procedure.

[251]Section 519 of Spanish Code of Civil Procedure. See Piñeiro (2016).

[252]Møgelvang-Hansen (2008: 3).

[253]Voet (2016: 3–4).

[254]Section 47/B(7)(c) of the 1998 Competition Act. See also Section 47/B(10)-(11) of the 1998 Competition Act.

[255]See Footnote 239.

is used. The CAT is not required to individualize the damages awarded: "[it] may make an award of damages (...) without undertaking an assessment of the amount of damages recoverable in respect of the claim of each represented person."[256]

As noted above, in a few Member States, judgments adopted in collective actions have limping res judicata effects.

In Hungary, it is not obvious if in opt-out proceedings available in competition and consumer protection law the judgment's res judicata effects extend to group members. The statutory text does not provide for this specifically. It deals only with the case when the group representative wins, not addressing the case of plaintiff failure. More importantly, group members are not parties to the collective action, hence, absent a specific provision, they should not be covered by the res judicata effects. Last but not least, the law provides that the collective action does not affect the consumer's right to pursue his rights individually.[257] All these suggest that while group members may "use" the judgment if the group representative prevails, they are not necessarily covered by the res judicata effect. However, this question has not been tested in judicial practice.

In the Greek consumer collective action, the judgment's res judicata effect extends to all (including absent) group members but only if the consumer association is, fully or partially, successful. In case the defendant does the comply with the judgment voluntarily, a consumer may request the court to issue a payment order for him.[258]

In Portugal, once a popular action is initiated, the court, after an appropriate public notice, sets a deadline for adherence or refusal of adherence. The popular action follows the opt-out principle[259]: silence infers adherence. However, the law shelters group members in various ways from the potentially detrimental consequences of res judicata. First, group members may opt out very late, until the end of the evidentiary procedure.[260] Second, the law erects two exceptions to the principle that the final judgment's res judicata effects extend to all group members who have not opted out: group members are not covered by the judgment's res judicata effects if the claim was rejected for lack of evidence, furthermore, the judge may decide to exempt group members from this effect considering the special characteristics of the case.[261]

Judgments in collective actions have limping res judicata effects also under French law, which has been above average creative as to the purview of res judicata in opt-out proceedings. The scheme appears to be a de facto opt-out system, although the

---

[256]Section 47/C(2) of the 1998 Competition Act.

[257]Section 92(8) of the Hungarian Competition Act; Section 38(7) of Act CLV of 1997 on Consumer Protection.

[258]Articles 10(20) of Law 2251/1994 on Consumers' Protection. See Emvalomenos (2016: 4) and European Parliament, Policy Department A: Economic and Scientific Policy, Directorate General for Internal Policies (2011: 25).

[259]Section 15 of the Portuguese Act on Popular Action.

[260]Antunes (2007: 20–21).

[261]Section 19 of the Portuguese Act on Popular Action. It is worthy of note that there is a theory in Portuguese doctrine which suggests that, due to considerations of constitutionality, only those legal consequences should have res judicata effects on group members which are beneficial to them. de Freitas (1998: 797, 809).

consumer's right to opt in is retained and can be exercised after the judgment is made. Accordingly, the judgment's res judicata effects extend to group members on the condition that they accept the award and get compensated: the judgment's res judicata effects cover only those group members who, after having been duly informed, expressly accept the judgment and the compensation.[262] Notwithstanding the conditional nature of the res judicata effects on individual group members, the judgment adopted at the end of the group action has a general preclusion effect against subsequent group actions initiated in the same case.[263]

5.7 Enforcement

Interestingly, although, as a matter of practice, this appears to be of crucial importance for the success of collective actions, in the vast majority of the systems, collective awards come under individual enforcement.[264]

Nonetheless, a handful of Member States made provisions for the collective enforcement of the judgment accruing from the collective action. In Malta, if the court awards compensation, it "may order the defendant to credit the amount due to a specific account held by the class representative and may give such orders, as it deems necessary, to the class representative for the effective distribution of that compensation among the class members."[265] In Belgium, collective awards and settlements are enforced under the supervision of a "collective claims settler", who can claim his costs and fees from the defendant.[266] In Slovenia, enforcement is carried out with the help of a collective redress manager.[267] In France, the money has to be paid directly to group members; however, the representative plaintiff may be authorized to enforce the award and distribute it among the members.[268] In the United Kingdom, in opt-out collective proceedings available in competition matters, the CAT may order that the damages be paid either to the representative plaintiff or any third person the CAT determines.[269] In opt-in proceedings, the damages are, in principle, to be paid

---

[262] Section 78 of Loi n° 2016-1547 du 18 novembre 2016 de modernisation de la justice du XXIe siècle, JORF n° 0269 du 19 novembre 2016 texte n° 1.

[263] Section 80 of Loi n° 2016-1547 du 18 novembre 2016 de modernisation de la justice du XXIe siècle, JORF n° 0269 du 19 novembre 2016 texte n° 1.

[264] Commission Report on the implementation of the Commission Recommendation of 11 June 2013 on common principles for injunctive and compensatory collective redress mechanisms in the Member States concerning violations of rights granted under Union law (2013/396/EU), COM(2018) 40 final, p 12. ("The enforcement of injunctions is generally carried out through the same measures irrespective of whether the injunctive order was issued in individual or collective proceedings").

[265] Article 18(3) of the Maltese Collective Proceedings Act.

[266] Section XVII.57-62 of the Belgian Code of Economic Law. See Voet (2016: 6–7).

[267] Article 43 of the Slovenian Law on Collective Actions.

[268] Sections 826-21-826-23 of the French Code of Civil Procedure; Lustin-Le Core (2016: 20).

[269] Section 47/C(3) of the 1998 Competition Act.

directly to group members unless the CAT decides otherwise (in which case they will be paid to the representative plaintiff or any third person the CAT determines).[270]

In Bulgaria, enforcement is managed by the group representative under court supervision. The court may require that the indemnification be collected in the name of one of the representatives or in an escrow account.[271] Furthermore, the court may convene a general meeting of all injured parties, which can decide on the manner of allocation or expenditure of the indemnification amount. This meeting is chaired by the judge and can adopt valid decisions if more than 6 injured parties attend.[272]

Normally, individual claims not enforced within the term of limitation remain with the defendant. However, for instance, in Portugal, if group members do not enforce the compensation awarded to them within three years, the claim accrues to the Ministry of Justice who is expected to use it to promote access to justice.[273] In securities law, the non-distributed part of the global compensation accrues to the respective financial sector's guarantee fund.[274] In case of antitrust damages actions, the non-distributed part may be used to pay for the promoters' costs of litigation, which would otherwise go uncompensated.[275] In the United Kingdom, in competition law opt-out collective actions, provision is made for unclaimed moneys: if the CAT "makes an award of damages in opt-out collective proceedings, any damages not claimed by the represented persons within a specified period must be paid to the charity for the time being prescribed by order made by the Lord Chancellor"[276] or the Secretary of State[277]; however, the CAT "may order that all or part of any damages not claimed by the represented persons within a specified period is instead to be paid to the representative in respect of all or part of the costs or expenses incurred by the representative in connection with the proceedings."[278]

5.8 Summary

Interestingly and counter-intuitively, 10 out of the 17 EU Member States that have adopted collective litigation schemes created systems based fully or partially on the opt-out principle (Belgium, Bulgaria, Denmark, France, Greece, Hungary, Portugal, Slovenia, Spain, and the United Kingdom) and only 7 of them stuck to the opt-in principle (Finland, Germany, Italy, Lithuania, Malta, Poland and Sweden). Accordingly, while it is true that in the vast majority of the Member States no opt-out collective

---

[270] Section 47/C(4) of the 1998 Competition Act.

[271] Section 387 of the Bulgarian Code on Civil Procedure.

[272] Section 388 of the Bulgarian Code on Civil Procedure.

[273] Section 22 of the Portuguese Act on Popular Action. Dias and Andrade e Castro (2016: 67).

[274] Section 31 of the Securities Code (Decree-Law 486/99 as revised).

[275] Section 19 of Law 23/2018 of 5 June on Antitrust Damages Actions.

[276] Section 47/C(5) of the 1998 Competition Act.

[277] Section 47/C(7) of the 1998 Competition Act.

[278] Section 47/C(6) of the 1998 Competition Act.

litigation is available, more than half of the countries that decided to create a special regime allowed representation without authorization in general or in given sectors.

Though a few countries have regimes of general scope, most European collective litigation systems have a limited ambit (such as consumer matters), reflecting the notion that collective actions should be limited to cases where they are highly needed. Some systems have used "leapfrogging" to extend the scheme to further sectors demonstrating the precautious approach of European legal systems as to collective litigation.

European collective litigation is normally subject to more stringent requirements than US class actions. The pre-conditions of collective litigation normally embrace those of US class action (numerousity, commonality, typicality and adequate representation) but quite a few systems go beyond these and require that collective litigation be expedient or superior to individual litigation and that the group be definable and group members identifiable by means of the group definition (especially in case the opt-out scheme is used).

The heroes of European collective litigation are governmental and non-governmental not-for-profit organizations (such as administrative agencies, the attorney general and consumer protection NGOs). Although standing is not reserved solely for them (in fact, in several Member States their standing operates in parallel to that of group members and only a few systems limit standing exclusively to public entities and non-profit organizations), they are expected to be the authors of collective actions (as law firms are in the US). There is a clear tendency to reserve "hard cases", which are difficult to manage and present a higher risk of abuse, to public entities and recognized civil organizations. According to European thinking, governmental and non-governmental not-for-profit organizations are assumed to be more attentive to the public interest than for-profit enterprises.

Although in opt-in systems group members expressly join the action, contrary to the group representative, they are formally not parties to the procedure. They are bound by the final judgment but in most systems, instead of them, it is the group representative who is liable for the prevailing defendant's legal costs.

Due to doctrinal and constitutional reasons, European opt-out class action legislation has been impregnated by the "only benefits" principle: the encroachment on party autonomy is justified by the fact that only benefits accrue to group members. European systems have been struggling remarkably with the implementation of this principle, producing innovative and idiosyncratic solutions. First, it is evident that in opt-out proceedings group members may not be liable for legal costs and the group representative should carry this burden. Second, it has been argued that party autonomy is restricted also if the individual group member is bound by an unfavorable judgment. Hence, in some European opt-out systems, the res judicata effects are limping in relation to group members. For instance, in France, group members are bound by the judgment only if they expressly accept the compensation. In Hungary, it is dubious if in opt-out proceedings available in competition and consumer protection matters the judgment's res judicata effect extends to group members. In Portugal, if the court decides for the defendant due to lack of evidence, the judgment will not be binding on group members; furthermore, as a general rule, if justified, the court may exempt group members of the judgment's res judicata effects.

Interestingly, although, as a matter of practice, this appears to be of crucial importance for the success of collective actions, in most systems, collective awards come under individual enforcement and only a handful of the Member States have made provision for collective enforcement.

The above modelling is crowned with the recent European proposal for a consumer collective action. In April 2018, the Commission proposed the adoption of a "representative action" in the field of consumer protection law.[279] The proposed directive is, in essence, based on the above common principles identified as the common core of the existing European mechanisms. Given that one third of the Member States has no collective action scheme, it is a significant virtue of the proposed directive that, if adopted, it will make consumer collective actions available in each and every Member State. On the other hand, at the present stage of the legislative process,[280] as a simple codification of the "collective action traditions common to the Member States", it is supposed to entail no landslide conceptual reform: it has a sectoral approach (consumer protection), rigorous pre-conditions, confers standing on qualified representative entities, maintains the "loser pays rule", rules out financial incentives, such as contingency fees and punitive damages and, last but not least, evades the dilemma of opt-in and opt-out through leaving the choice to Member States.[281]

References

Afferni G (2016) Opt-in class actions in Italy: why are they failing? J Eur Tort Law 7(1):82–100
Almoguera J, Perete C, de la Villa C (2004) National report: Spain. In: Study on the conditions of claims for damages in case of infringement of EC competition rules. Ashurst. http://ec.europa.eu/competition/antitrust/actionsdamages/national_reports/spain_en.pdf. Accessed 20 Apr 2019
Andrews N (2001) Multi-party proceedings in England: representative and group actions. Duke J Comp Int Law 11(2):249–267
Antunes HS (2007) Class actions, group litigation & other forms of collective litigation. Portuguese report. http://globalclassactions.stanford.edu/sites/default/files/documents/Portugal_National_Report.pdf. Accessed 20 Apr 2019
Bosters T (2017) Collective redress and private international law in the EU. TMC Asser Press, The Hague

---

[279]Proposal for a Directive on representative actions for the protection of the collective interests of consumers, and repealing Directive 2009/22/EC, COM(2018) 184 final. See European Parliament legislative resolution of 26 March 2019 on the proposal for a directive of the European Parliament and of the Council on representative actions for the protection of the collective interests of consumers, and repealing Directive 2009/22/EC (COM(2018)0184–C8-0149/2018–2018/0089(COD)).

[280]https://oeil.secure.europarl.europa.eu/oeil/popups/ficheprocedure.do?reference=2018/0089(COD)&l=en. Accessed 20 April 2019.

[281]See Footnote 14.

British Institute of International and Comparative Law (2017) State of collective redress in the EU in the context of the implementation of the Commission Recommendation. JUST/2016/JCOO/FW/CIVI/0099. Nov 2017. https://www.biicl.org/documents/1881_StudyontheStateofCollectiveRedress.pdf?showdocument=1. Accessed 20 Apr 2019

Caponi R (2011a) Class action. Il nuovo volto della tutela collettiva in Italia. Giuffrè

Caponi R (2011b) Collective redress in Europe: current developments of "class action" suits in Italy. Zeitschrift für Zivilprozess International 16:61–77

de Ávila Ruiz-Peinado FR (2016) Spanish antitrust private enforcement: enhancing consumer collective redress. Working Paper IE Law School. AJ8-229-I 20-01-2016. https://papers.ssrn.com/sol3/papers.cfm?abstract_id=2603265. Accessed 20 Apr 2019

de Cabiedes Hidalgo PB (2007a) Spanish legislation on collective actions: selected excerpts. http://globalclassactions.stanford.edu/sites/default/files/documents/Spain_Legislation.pdf. Accessed 20 Apr 2019

de Cabiedes Hidalgo PB (2007b) Group litigation in Spain. National report. http://globalclassactions.stanford.edu/sites/default/files/documents/spain_national_report.pdf. Accessed 20 Apr 2019

de Freitas JL (1998) A acção popular ao serviço do ambiente. In: Varela A, Freitas do Amaral D, Miranda J, Canotilho JJG (eds) Ab uno ad omnes / 75 anos da Coimbra Editora. Coimbra Editora, Coimbra

Dias SF, Andrade e Castro M (2016) Portugal. In: Feldman JS, Anderson JE (eds) Class actions—getting the deal through 2017. Law Business Research, London, pp 65–67

Emvalomenos D (2016) Greece. EU collective redress project 2016, Oxford, 12–13 Dec 2016. https://www.law.ox.ac.uk/sites/files/oxlaw/greece.docx. Accessed 20 Apr 2019

Ernesto C, Fernando B (eds) (2012) La nuova class action a tutela dei consumatori e degli utenti. CEDAM

Ervo L (2016) Opt-in is out and opt-out is in: dimensions based on nordic options and the Commission's Recommendation. In: Hess B, Bergström M, Storskrubb E (eds) EU civil justice: current issues and future outlook. Hart Publishing, Oxford, pp 185–200

Ervo L, Persson AH, Lindblom T (Unknown) Sweden. http://www.collectiveredress.org/collective-redress/reports/sweden/caselaw. Accessed 20 Apr 2019

European Parliament, Policy Department A: Economic and Scientific Policy, Directorate General for Internal Policies (2011) Overview of existing collective redress schemes in EU Member States. IP/A/IMCO/NT/2011-16, PE464.433. July 2011. http://www.europarl.europa.eu/document/activities/cont/201107/20110715ATT24242/20110715ATT24242EN.pdf. Accessed 20 Apr 2018

European Parliament, Policy Department for Citizens' Rights and Constitutional Affairs, Directorate General for Internal Policies of the Union (2018) Collective redress in the Member States of the European Union. PE 608.829. Oct 2018. http://www.europarl.europa.eu/RegData/etudes/STUD/2018/608829/IPOL_STU(2018)608829_EN.pdf. Accessed 20 Apr 2018

Fairgrieve D, Howells G (2009) Collective redress procedures—European debates. Int Compar Law Quart 58(2):379–409

Ferro MS (2015) Collective redress: will Portugal show the way? J Eur Compet Law Pract 6(5):299–300

Gomez F, Gili M (2008) Country-report: Spain. In: Evaluation of the effectiveness and efficiency of collective redress mechanisms in the European Union. Civic Consulting & Oxford Economics

Halfmeier A (2017) Musterfeststellungsklage: Nicht gut, aber besser als nichts. Z Recht 50(7):201–205

Halfmeier A, Feess E (2012) The German capital markets model case act (KapMuG)—a European role model for increasing the efficiency of capital markets? Analysis and suggestions for reform. http://ssrn.com/abstract=1684528. Accessed 20 Apr 2019

Hensler DR (2017) From sea to shining sea: how and why class actions are spreading globally. Univ Kansas Law Rev 65:965–988

Hodges C (2009) From class actions to collective redress: a revolution in approach to compensation. Civ Just Quart 28:41–66

Hodges C (2010) Collective redress in Europe: the new model. Civ Justice Quart 29(3):370–395

Juška Z (Unknown) Country report: class actions in Lithuania. http://globalclassactions.stanford.edu/sites/default/files/documents/LITHUANIA.pdf. Accessed 20 Apr 2019

Katzarsky A, Georgiev G (2012) Bulgaria. In: Dodds-Smith I, Brown A (eds) The international comparative legal guide to class & group actions. Global Legal Group, London (Chapter 11)

Kiurunen P (2012) Finland. In: Karlsgodt PG (ed) World class actions: a guide to group and representative actions around the globe. Oxford University Press, Oxford, pp 214–228 (Chapter 8)

Krans B (2014) The Dutch Act on collective settlement of mass damages. Pac McGeorge Glob Bus Deve Law J 27(2):281–301

Laffineur J, Renier G (2016) L'action en réparation collective: un premier état des lieux deux ans après son introduction en droit belge. Droit de la consommation—Consumentenrecht (DCCR) 112:3–20

Lindblom PH (1997) Individual litigation and mass justice: a Swedish perspective and proposal on group actions in civil procedure. Am J Comp Law 45(4):805–831

Lindblom PH (2007) National report: group litigation in Sweden, the globalization of class actions. http://globalclassactions.stanford.edu/sites/default/files/documents/Sweden_National_Report.pdf. Accessed 20 Apr 2019

Lindblom PH (2008) Globalization of class action. National report: group litigation in Sweden. Update paper sections 2.5 and 3. http://globalclassactions.stanford.edu/sites/default/files/documents/Sweden_Update_paper_Nov%20-08.pdf. Accessed 20 Apr 2019

Lustin-Le Core C (2016) France. In: Feldman JS, Anderson JE (eds) Class actions—getting the deal through 2017. Law Bus Res, London

Magnier V (2007) Class actions, group litigation & other forms of collective litigation. http://globalclassactions.stanford.edu/sites/default/files/documents/France_National_Report.pdf. Accessed 20 Apr 2019

Magnier V, Alleweldt R (2008) Country-report: France. In: Evaluation of the effectiveness and efficiency of collective redress mechanisms in the European Union. Civic Consulting & Oxford Economics

Markova T (2015) Collective claims: ex ante analysis of claim submissions in Bulgaria (Колективните искове: екс анте анализ на предявяването им в България). Econ Soc Altern (Икономически и социални алтернативи) 1:142–152

Møgelvang-Hansen P (2008) Country-report: Denmark. In: Evaluation of the effectiveness and efficiency of collective redress mechanisms in the European Union. Civic Consulting & Oxford Economics

Momège C, Bessot N (2004) National report: France. In: Study on the conditions of claims for damages in case of infringement of EC competition rules. Ashurst. http://ec.europa.eu/competition/antitrust/actionsdamages/national_reports/france_en.pdf. Accessed 20 Apr 2019

Mulheron R (2009) The case for an opt-out class action for European member states: a legal and empirical analysis. Columbia J Eur Law 15:409–453

Mulheron R (2014) The class action in common law legal systems: a comparative perspective. Oxford University Press, Oxford

Nagy CI (2015) The European collective redress debate after the European commission's recommendation: one step forward, two steps back? Maastricht J Eur Comp Law 22(4):530–552

Neumann K-A, Magnusson LW (2011) Pour une class-action européenne dans le droit de la concurrence. Revue québécoise de droit international 24(2):149–181

Nielsen PA, Linhart K (2012) Danish class actions—a European model? Int J Priv Law 5(3):229–242

Nordh R (2001) Group actions in Sweden: reflections on the purpose of civil litigation, the need for reforms, and a forthcoming proposal. Duke J Comp Int Law 11:381–404

Paris SO (2015) Private antitrust enforcement: a new era for collective redress. Yearb Antitrust Regul Stud 8(12):11–32

Persson AH (2008) Country-report: Sweden. In: Evaluation of the effectiveness and efficiency of collective redress mechanisms in the European Union. https://pure.uva.nl/ws/files/4314114/61401_294507.pdf. Accessed 20 Apr 2019

Persson AH (2012) Collective enforcement: European prospects in light of the Swedish experience. In: Wrbka S, van Uytsel S, Siems MM (eds) Collective actions: enhancing access to justice and reconciling multilayer interests?. Cambridge University Press, Cambridge, pp 341–363

Pettersson LT, Lindeborg SP, Giolito MP (2004) National report: Sweden. In: Study on the conditions of claims for damages in case of infringement of EC competition rules. Ashurst. http://ec.europa.eu/competition/antitrust/actionsdamages/national_reports/sweden_en.pdf. Accessed 20 Apr 2019

Piñeiro CL (2013) Recomendación de la Comisión Europea sobre los Principios comunes aplicables a los mecanismos de recurso colectivo de cesación o de indemnización en los Estados miembros en caso de violación de los derechos reconocidos por el Derecho de la Unión Europea (Estrasburgo, 11 de junio de 2013). Revista española de derecho internacional 65(2):395–399

Piñeiro LC (2015) La construcción del mercado interior y el recurso colectivo de consumidores. In: Rosa FEdl (ed) La protección del consumidor en dos espacios de integración: Europa y América. Una perspectiva de derecho internacional, europeo y comparado. Tirant lo Blanch, Valencia, pp 1055–1096

Piñeiro LC (2016) Consumer collective arbitration in Spain. what's in a name? In: Hanotiau B, Schwarz EA (eds) Class and group actions in arbitration. Dossiers ICC Institute of World Business Law, Paris, pp 88–104

Principe G (2012) Italian class actions. An update. http://globalclassactions.stanford.edu/sites/default/files/documents/Italian%20Class%20Actions%20Principe.pdf. Accessed 20 Apr 2019

Renier G (2018) L'action en réparation collective pour les consommateurs élargie aux PME. Droit de la consommation—Consumentenrecht (DCCR) (118):141–143

Rodger BJ (2015) The consumer rights act 2015 and collective redress for competition law infringements in the UK: a class act? J Antitrust Enforcement 3(2):258–286

Rossi L, Ferro MS (2013) Private enforcement of competition law in Portugal (II): actio popularis—facts, fictions and dreams. Revista de Concorrência e Regulação 4(1):35–87

Schäfer H-B (2018) Musterfeststellungsklage: Ein Schritt in die richtige Richtung. Wirtschaftsdienst 98(7):456

Sherman EF (2002) Group litigation under foreign legal systems: variations and alternatives to American class action. DePaul Law Review 52(2):401–432

Silvestri E (2007a) Consumers' collective actions: an update on Italian draft legislation. http://globalclassactions.stanford.edu/sites/default/files/documents/Italian_National_Report_supplemtary.pdf. Accessed 20 Apr 2019

Silvestri E (2007b) The globalization of class actions. Italian report. http://globalclassactions.stanford.edu/sites/default/files/documents/Italian_National_Report_0.pdf. Accessed 20 Apr 2019

Silvestri E (2008) The Italian "collective action for damages": an update. http://globalclassactions.stanford.edu/sites/default/files/documents/Italian_Collective_Action_for_Damages.pdf. Accessed 20 Apr 2019

Sladič J (2018) A new model of civil litigation in Slovenia: is the Slovenian judiciary prepared for the challenges presented by the new law on collective actions? In: Uzelac A, van Rhee CHR (eds) Transformation of civil justice: unity and diversity. Springer, Heidelberg, pp 213–227

Stadler A (2009) Der Gewinnsbschöpfungsanspruch: eine Variante des Private enforcement? In: Augenhofer S (ed) Die Europäisierung des Kartell- und Lauterkeitsrechts. Mohr Siebeck, Tübingen, pp 117–140

Stadler A (2015) Die Umsetzung der Kommissionsempfehlung zum kollektiven Rechtsschutz. Zeitschrift für die gesamte Privatrechtswissenschaft 1(1):61–84

Staudt C (2019) Note—Dieselgate: entre solution juridique et réaction émotionnelle. Revue Générale de Droit Civil Belge 49(3):146–158

Steinberger E (2016) Die Gruppenklage im Kapitalmarktrecht: Vorschläge zur Weiterentwicklung des Kapitalanleger-Musterverfahrensgesetzes (KapMuG). Nomos, Baden-Baden

Szalai Á (2014) Kollektív keresetek joggazdaságtana. Iustum Aequum Salutare X(1):163–181

Szalai Á (2017) Társult perek: nyitott kérdések és joggazdaságtani elemzés. Eljárásjogi Szemle 2(3):22–31

Tortell I, (2008) Country-report: Portugal. In: Evaluation of the effectiveness and efficiency of collective redress mechanisms in the European Union. Civic Consulting & Oxford Economics

Trstenjak V (2015) Les mécanismes de recours collectif et leur importance pour la protection des consommateurs. In: Tizzano A, Rosas A, de Lapuerta RS, Lenaerts K, Kokott J (eds) La Cour de justice de l'Union européenne sous la présidence de Vassilios Skouris (2003–2015): liber amicorum Vassilios Skouris. Bruylant, Bruxelles, pp 681–696

Udvary S (2012) Some remarks on class action in antitrust cases in the US and EU. Versenytükör 8(2):36–41

Udvary S (2018) A közérdekű és társult perek a polgári perrendtartásban. Jogtudományi Közlöny 73(5):221–230

Välimäki M (2007) Introducing class actions in Finland—lawmaking without economic analysis. http://ssrn.com/abstract=1261623. Accessed on 20 Apr 2019

Veljanovski C (2019) Collective certification in UK competition law: commonality, costs and funding. World Compet 42(1):121–138

Viitanen K (2007) Collective litigation in Finland. http://globalclassactions.stanford.edu/sites/default/files/documents/Finland_National_Report.pdf. Accessed 20 Apr 2019

Viitanen K (2008) Country-report: Finland. In: Evaluation of the effectiveness and efficiency of collective redress mechanisms in the European Union. Civic Consulting & Oxford Economics

Voet S (2016) Class action developments in Belgium. http://globalclassactions.stanford.edu/default/files/documents/BELGIUM.pdf. Accessed 20 Apr 2019

Weimann M (2018) Kollektiver Rechtsschutz: Ein Memorandum der Praxis. Walter de Gruyter, Berlin

Werlauff E (2008) Class actions in Denmark—from 2008. http://globalclassactions.stanford.edu/sites/default/files/documents/Demark_National_Report.pdf. Accessed 20 Apr 2019

Zdolšek S, Jurca I, Zdolsek K (2018) Slovenia. In: Campbell AN (ed) Cartel regulation—getting the deal through 2019. Law Business Research, London, pp 228–233

Chapter 6
Conclusions

The European history of collective actions started roughly three decades ago. While collective litigation proved to be one of the most successful export products of American legal scholarship, it has been very likely also one of the legal transplantations that generated the most heated debates. This process, not devoid of scare-mongering and legislative hesitation, has resulted in a landscape where 17 out of 28 Member States have adopted a special regime for collective actions. This evolution is crowned with the Commission's recent proposal for a consumer collective action.[1]

Though US class actions have been a point of reference, collective litigation has been fundamentally reshaped during the European transplantation. Not surprisingly, this metamorphosis has been due to European law's discrepant mental attitude and diverging regulatory environment.

First of all, in contrast with US law's notion that private plaintiffs (both individual and collective) may function as a "private attorney general", European collective actions have no public policy role but are confined to serving a purely compensatory function. In Europe, even the proponents of opt-out class actions tend to disallow its possible public policy function and to conceive its role purely as providing an effective remedy to group members.

Second, it has been evident that the operation of collective litigation, due to the absence of certain contextual doctrines, will differ sharply on the two sides of the Atlantic. In fact, the diverging regulatory environment (e.g. the absence of contingency fees, the American rule on attorney's fees, punitive and treble damages in Europe) takes off the edge of the European criticism against the introduction of class actions, which is largely, if not fully, attributable to the above contextual concepts.

---

[1] Proposal for a Directive on representative actions for the protection of the collective interests of consumers, and repealing Directive 2009/22/EC, COM(2018) 184 final. See European Parliament legislative resolution of 26 March 2019 on the proposal for a directive of the European Parliament and of the Council on representative actions for the protection of the collective interests of consumers, and repealing Directive 2009/22/EC (COM(2018)0184–C8-0149/2018–2018/0089(COD)).

© The Author(s) 2019
C. I. Nagy, *Collective Actions in Europe*,
SpringerBriefs in Law, https://doi.org/10.1007/978-3-030-24222-0_6

Third, due to the dissimilar regulatory environment, in Europe, collective litigation raises a good number of regulatory issues that simply do not emerge in the country of origin. Because of the American rule, the plaintiffs' liability for legal costs is not an issue in the US, while it is a central question in Europe. Litigation finance is a crucial problem in Europe, contrary to the US, where various means of general application (such as contingency fees, super-compensatory damages, one-way costs shifting in certain fields) are available to incite and reward those who fund litigation and these are equally available in individual and collective actions.

Fourth, the taboo of party autonomy has had a profound impact on European systems, especially opt-out schemes. This entailed the emergence of the "only benefits" principle concerning collective proceedings' effects on group members.

All these differences resulted in a system à l'européenne.

6.1   Collective Actions Are Needed in Europe to Ensure Access to Justice and Effectiveness of the Law

Small claims face hurdles that may prevent individual enforcement and lead to suboptimal enforcement.[2] Collective litigation may make litigation possible also in cases where individual litigation would not be economically rational. Collective actions may entail cost-savings due to economies of scale and may tackle the problem of positive externalities. Through making the enforcement of small-value claims a reality, it ensures access to justice and effectiveness of the law. Nonetheless, collective litigation necessitates regulatory intervention, since, due to the high costs of group organization, it would not work spontaneously and, accordingly, the law has to tackle the problem of organizational costs so as to make the enforcement of these claims a reality.

The costs and risks may make litigation economically unreasonable even in well-founded cases (the expected costs may be higher than the expected value).

First, non-recoverable legal costs may deter litigation. Although in Europe legal costs are, in principle and with some restrictions, borne by the losing party, the winning party cannot shift the legal costs in full. The proof and documentation of the legal expenses may be difficult; the law may restrict the amount of the attorney's fees that can be shifted onto the losing party; the claim's enforcement may give rise to some practically unrecoverable expenses. Furthermore, certain expenses cannot be shifted onto the losing party (these costs are legally not shiftable). Examples are inconveniences related to litigation and the time the claimant spends on the claim. Obviously, such expenses may emerge in any matter, but in respect of small claims these costs are comparably much higher given the small pecuniary value involved.

Second, the costs of preliminary legal assessment may also dissuade the plaintiff. Although, theoretically, these may be regarded as shiftable expenses (as they emerge in relation to litigation), information shortage pertains to such situations.

---

[2]For a detailed elaboration of the analysis set forth in this section see Nagy (2013: 469–498).

The preliminary legal assessment occurs at a stage where the claimant has no information about his chances, so he has to take into account that he may have to pay even if there is no reason to sue.

Third, in matters involving small claims, the value at stake is small and legal costs are, in comparison to the claim's value, very high, hence, a relatively trivial probability of failure may make the balance of litigation negative. The higher the legal costs are in relation to the claim's value, the better this risk crops out. As a matter of practice, litigation inevitably involves some risk and almost all claims have immanent hazards.

Collective actions have certain advantages that make the enforcement of small claims possible in cases where numerous persons are damaged by the same illegal act. Although damages are small for each individual (what may make litigation unreasonable), collective damages (the sum of various individuals' damages) are high.

The merit of collective actions can be attributed to two virtues: economies of scale[3] and tackling external economic effects (externalities). Joint litigation may entail economies of scale and is susceptible of doing away with the external economic effects individual litigation may cause. This is due to the fact that the enforcement of individual small claims may have significant common costs.[4] Although it is true that this is a general advantage of joint litigation (that is, it may equally emerge in cases where the claims are not of small value), in case of small claims, the cost-savings are comparably higher than in case of huge claims.

In related matters, litigation costs are often not commensurable to the number of claimants, since certain expenses (testimonies, deliberation of liability and so on) emerge only once.[5] A substantial part of the legal costs may be fixed costs, which emerge independently of the number of the claimants, while the rest may be made up of variable costs, which are affected by the number of claimants. If the loss is caused by the same wrong, there may be common (fixed) costs; and if these are significant in comparison to individual costs, collective actions may be cost-effective.

Individual litigation may entail positive external effects (externalities), conferring advantages on other class members they did not pay for. The difference between the expected costs and the expected value may be negative on individual level but positive on group (or social) level. Since the individual litigator does not benefit from the positive external economic effects enjoyed by other group members (that is, these benefits are not internalized), this may lead to sub-optimal litigation. Although one might argue that test cases can effectively substitute collective litigation, this is refuted by the fact that test cases may entail free-riding: non-active group members may free-ride on the efforts of the individual litigator who started the test case.

The reason why collective litigation does not occur, at least not on a large scale, spontaneously, notwithstanding the several traditional legal tools (joinder of parties,[6]

---

[3]See e.g. Ulen (2011: 185, 187).
[4]See Bone (2003: 261–265).
[5]Ulen (2011: 185, 187).
[6]Nagy (2011: 163).

assignment of claims to an entity founded by group members)[7] that may be used to organize the group, is the cost of group organization. These costs may be very high, in some cases even prohibitive,[8] and traditional legal tools are not tailored to the needs of collective litigation, thus increasing the costs of group management.[9]

6.2 European Objections and Fears Against the Opt-Out System: Superego, Ego and Id

In the European scholarly discourse, resistance against US class actions has been predominantly dogmatic (constitutional doctrine of party autonomy) but, subconsciously, backed by the settled European thinking that the enforcement of public policy is the prerogative of the state and may not be privatized. Indeed, the "Copernican turn" of opt-out collective litigation interferes with the ontological principles of European civil procedure: while a civil action traditionally centers around the claim, in the US class action the claims center around the procedure.

European traditionalism has been often wrapped up in constitutional parlance, but the arguments against class actions' constitutional conformity have found no reflection in the constitutional case-law. This suggests that while certain limits do apply, opt-out mechanisms are not outright unconstitutional and they may be constitutionally warranted in small value cases, which would very likely not be brought to court anyway.

The scholarship is replete with pieces supporting the introduction of the opt-out model in Europe. Disregarding the misconceived references to legal tradition and the phobia of foreign legal solutions, one can rarely find any analysis convincingly demonstrating that the introduction of the opt-out model in Europe would lead to a litigation boom, settlements forced out by black-mailing and abuses.

The alleged repercussions of opt-out collective litigation in the US would not occur when this regulatory mechanism is transplanted into a European environment. Legal rules do not operate in a vacuum but are part of a legal, social, cultural, and economic environment. US law contains a large set of institutions that catalyze the opt-out class action's operation. In Europe, failing this catalyzing environment, the alleged excesses of the US practice are not to be expected. This conclusion is underpinned by the limited European empirical evidence concerning opt-out collective actions and by the examples of foreign legal systems that are comparable to the European regulatory environment and have adopted US-style class action schemes (Australia, Canada, Latin-American countries).

As demonstrated above, in class action cases group representatives have the very same black-mailing potential (if any) as the plaintiff in an individual action. The US litigation landscape is shaped by legal institutions like punitive and treble damages,

---

[7]Id.

[8]Ulen (2011: 185, 191).

[9]For a detailed analysis, see Nagy (2013: 469, 478–479).

the "American rule" on attorney's fees, one-way-cost shifting in certain cases, contingency fees, entrepreneurial law firms and litigious attitudes. This regulatory and social environment, which is responsible for what many Europeans attribute to class actions, is completely missing in Europe.

6.3 Transatlantic Perspectives: Comparative Law Framing

The regulatory and social environments of collective actions differ considerably on the two sides of the Atlantic. Contrary to the US, "entrepreneurial lawyering" is virtually missing in Europe, contingency fees are either prohibited (or available with restrictions) or, even if legal, are normally not available in the market; active client-acquiring and lawyer advertisements are banned or heavily restricted in most EU Member States. The "American rule" and especially one-way cost-shifting, as provided by various American protective statutes, are unknown to European jurisdictions, which traditionally follow the two-way cost-shifting rule. Super-compensatory damages are not available in Europe, with some narrow and insignificant exceptions in a handful of common law jurisdictions. The generous US rules on pre-trial discovery have similarly no counter-part.

These differences have twofold consequences. First, the operation and impact of European collective actions differ considerable from their American ancestor due to the absence of the above pro-plaintiff incentives. Second, European legislators have to address quite a few regulatory issues that do not emerge in the US.

Both theoretical analysis and empirical data clearly suggest that the purported negative repercussions of opt-out collective litigation (US class action) would not emerge if this regulatory mechanism is introduced in Europe. The theoretical arguments and the brief account of empirical evidence suggest that, whereas the relatively short time that has elapsed since the wide-spread appearance of these mechanisms (both opt-in and opt-out systems) in Europe does not enable us to predict the long-run consequences, it is safe to say that opt-out collective proceedings would trigger no litigation boom in Europe. This conclusion is underpinned also by the empirical experiments of Australia and Canada, which have a regulatory environment different from the US in some of the relevant aspects.

The transplantation of collective actions into a European legal and social environment raises an array of novel regulatory questions.

European legal systems lack the counterparts of US legal institutions that facilite litigation through the provision of financial incentives (one-way cost-shifting, contingency fees and punitive damages), making litigation finance a crucial regulatory issue. Unfortunately, European collective action laws have failed to settle or even address this problem: while they ruled out the American institutions that stimulate class actions, they failed to replace these with appropriate substitutes. Arguably, European collective actions have little chance to become effective and self-sustaining, if, one way or another, appropriate financial incentives or funding are not provided for to ensure that the group representative gets compensated (receives a premium) for running financial risks in the interest of the group. Economically speaking, the group representative's expected income and expected costs cannot be equilibrated in the absence of an appropriate risk premium or non-profit-oriented (public) funding and, hence, he may be incited to espouse the group members' claims if he is compensated for the risks he runs when engaging in collective litigation.

The effectiveness and widespread use of collective litigation and the potential for abuse and adverse effects are inversely proportionate to each other. On the one hand, economically speaking, the group representative's expected income and expected costs cannot be equilibrated in the absence of an appropriate risk premium. On the other hand, such a risk premium would move the European regulatory environment from its current position towards US law. The European legislator or legislators need to find the point of equilibrium where the marginal benefit of effective enforcement equals the marginal cost of abuse and adverse effects. Alternatively, they may refuse to provide a risk premium to the group representative; empirical evidence shows that, mainly due to non-economic considerations, collective litigation may also be workable in the absence of a risk-premium, albeit on a low-key level.

While in US class actions group representatives, due to the American rule, are not responsible for the defendant's attorney's fees even if the class action fails, in Europe the principle of two-way cost-shifting prevails, raising the regulatory question of allocation both in opt-in and opt-out systems. It is generally accepted that the opt-out scheme's constitutionality may be preserved only if group members are freed from all liability and the group representative runs the full risk as to legal costs. This makes the "only benefits" principle, which prevails in opt-out systems, a peculiar element of the European collective action's architecture. The strongest argument for "representation without authorization" and against the allegation that opt-out collective actions encroach on party autonomy is that only benefits may accrue to group members, so it would be redundant to require express authorization. Hence, these systems were worked out in a way that group members run no risk as to legal costs; some of them also provide that group members are covered by the final judgment's res judicata effects only if they expressly accept it or if that is in their interest.

European collective actions are not meant to have a public policy role and their function is limited to ensuring a compensatory remedy for group members. As the concept of "private attorney general" is completely alien to European legal systems and the general attitude is that financial incentives may give an unacceptable stimulus, for-profit entities' aptness to serve the public interest is normally received with doubt. This explains why in Europe standing has been often limited to public entities and non-profit organizations.

6.4   European Models of Collective Actions: A Transsystemic Overview

Interestingly and counter-intuitively, 10 out of the 17 EU Member States that have adopted collective litigation schemes created systems based fully or partially on the opt-out principle (Belgium, Bulgaria, Denmark, France, Greece, Hungary, Portugal, Slovenia, Spain and the United Kingdom) and only 7 of them stuck to the opt-in principle (Finland, Germany, Italy, Lithuania, Malta, Poland and Sweden). Accordingly, while it is true that opt-out collective litigation is not available in the vast majority of the Member States, those countries which decided to create a special regime allowed representation without authorization in general or in given sectors.

Though a few countries have regimes of general scope, most European collective litigation systems have a limited ambit (such as consumer matters), reflecting the notion that collective actions should be limited to cases where they are highly needed. Some systems have used "leapfrogging" to extend the scheme to further sectors demonstrating the precautious approach of European legal systems as to collective litigation.

European collective litigation is normally subject to more stringent requirements than US class actions. The pre-conditions of collective litigation normally embrace those of US class action (numerousity, commonality, typicality and adequate representation) but quite a few systems go beyond these requiring that collective litigation be expedient or superior to individual litigation and that the group be definable and group members identifiable by means of the group definition (especially in case the opt-out scheme is used).

The heroes of European collective litigation are governmental and non-governmental not-for-profit organizations (such as administrative agencies, the attorney general and consumer protection NGOs). Although standing is not reserved solely for them (in fact, in several Member States their standing operates in parallel to that of group members and only a few systems limit standing exclusively to public entities and non-profit organizations), they are expected to be the authors of collective actions (as law-firms are in the US). There is a clear tendency to reserve "hard cases", which are difficult to manage and present a higher risk of abuse, for public entities and recognized civil organizations. According to European thinking, governmental and non-governmental not-for-profit organizations are assumed to be more attentive to the public interest than for-profit enterprises.

Although in opt-in systems group members expressly join the action, contrary to the group representative, they are formally not parties to the procedure. They are bound by the final judgment but in most systems, instead of them, it is the group representative who is liable for the prevailing defendant's legal costs.

As noted above, due to doctrinal and constitutional reasons, European opt-out collective action legislation has been impregnated by the "only benefits" principle: the encroachment on party autonomy is justified by the fact that only benefits accrue to group members. European systems have been struggling remarkably with the implementation of this principle, producing innovative and idiosyncratic solutions. First, it is evident that in opt-out proceedings group members may not be liable for legal costs and the group representative should carry this burden. Second, it has been argued that party autonomy is restricted also if the individual group member is bound by an unfavorable judgment. Hence, in some European systems, the res judicata effect is limping in relation to group members. For instance, in France, group members are bound by the judgment only if they expressly accept the compensation. In Hungary, it is dubious if in opt-out proceedings available in competition and consumer protection matters the judgment's res judicata effects extend to group members. In Portugal, if the court decides for the defendant due to lack of evidence, the judgment will not be binding on group members; furthermore, as a general rule, if justified, the court may exempt group members of the judgment's res judicata effects.

Interestingly, although, as a matter of practice, this appears to be of crucial importance for the success of collective actions, in most systems, collective awards come under individual enforcement and only a handful of the Member States have made provisions for collective enforcement.

The above modelling is crowned with the recent European proposal for a consumer collective action. In April 2018, the Commission proposed the adoption of a "representative action" in the field of consumer protection law.[10] The proposed directive is virtually based on the above common principles based on the common core of the existing European mechanisms. Given that one third of the Member States has no collective action scheme at all, it is a significant virtue of the proposed directive that, if adopted, it will make consumer collective actions available in each and every Member State. On the other hand, at the present stage of the legislative process,[11] as a simple codification of the "collective action traditions common to the Member States", it is supposed to entail no landslide conceptual reform: it has a sectoral approach (consumer protection), rigorous pre-conditions, confers standing on qualified representative entities, maintains the "loser pays rule", rules out financial incentives, such as contingency fees and punitive damages and, last but not least, evades the dilemma of opt-in and opt-out through leaving the choice to Member States.[12]

---

[10] See Footnote 1.

[11] https://oeil.secure.europarl.europa.eu/oeil/popups/ficheprocedure.do?reference=2018/0089(COD)&l=en. Accessed 20 April 2019.

[12] Article 6.

6.5   Closing Thoughts: "Small Money, Small Football, Big Money, Big Football"[13]

The debate in Europe on "whether to opt out or not to opt out" has become fairly repetitious. Although this is a truly important issue, it seems to be outdated in a certain sense and is losing weight in the online age where group members can simply "click in". The success of collective actions hinges on funding,[14] including the question of risk premium. An opt-out system does lessen the group's organizational costs significantly and makes collective actions possible in cases where such costs proved to be prohibitive. However, collective actions cannot be truly effective without appropriate funding. This does not mean that no cases would be brought to court; this means that the practical success of collective actions would not be as considerable as it should be. This is underpinned by both economic analysis and experience: in Europe, there are (relatively) successful opt-in and unsuccessful opt-out systems. Without slighting the relevance of the opt-out-opt-in controversy, it seems that, as a matter of fact, the pivotal question of collective actions is funding. It is not a co-incidence (that is, not a mere correlation but causation) that the world's most successful collective action mechanism provides for appropriate funding in the form of a variety of legal institutions (for example, punitive damages, treble damages, one-way cost shifting).

However, it has to be stressed that the need for a risk premium is certainly not an argument against the introduction of an opt-out system, especially, because the group representative may espouse the collective proceedings also for non-economic reasons. Collective actions can work without a risk-premium but their intensity will be lower than it could be.

As noted above, the enforcement of collective claims, like the enforcement of individual claims, hinges on costs and financing. However, it is an important difference between individual and collective actions that, in the latter case, there are considerable organizational costs, which, in certain matters, may prove to be prohibitive. Furthermore, due to the involvement of a third party (group representative),[15] financing may become more complicated. Group representatives are expected to take over the group's case and to invest in the business of someone else, without having a clear prospect of reward. Even if reasonable expenses are remunerated (compensating the representative for the cost he incurs in the interest of group members), group representatives will be disinclined to undertake the burden of group representation, unless they are secured a risk premium or receive public funding. While European legal systems reject those legal institutions of US law that afford a risk premium to group representatives and that make the US class action operational, they fail to

---

[13]Ferenc Puskás, Hungarian Footballer, Captain of the Golden Team.

[14]Cf. British Institute of International and Comparative Law (2017: 18–20).

[15]Though the group representative may be a group member, he still qualifies as a third party as to the claims of the rest of the group.

suggest alternative measures that could handle this problem. Nonetheless, one way or another (through a risk premium or public funding) group representatives have to be funded. At the end of the day, someone has to pay the piper ….

References

Bone R (2003) Civil procedure: the economics of civil procedure. Foundation Press
British Institute of International and Comparative Law (2017) State of collective redress in the EU in the context of the implementation of the Commission Recommendation. JUST/2016/JCOO/FW/CIVI/0099, Nov 2017. https://www.biicl.org/documents/1881_StudyontheStateofCollectiveRedress.pdf?showdocument=1. Accessed 20 Apr 2019
Nagy CI (2011) A csoportos igényérvényesítés gazdaságtana és lehetőségei a magyar jogban. Jogtudományi Közlöny 66(3):163–174
Nagy CI (2013) Comparative collective redress from a law and economics perspective: without risk there is no reward! Columbia J Eur Law 19(3):469–498
Ulen TS (2011) An introduction to the law and economics of class action litigation. Eur J Law Econ 32:185–203